SO YOU THINK YOU KNOW
YOU KNOW
HIS DARK
MATERIALS?

Clive Gifford

Hodder
Children's
Books

a division of Hodder Headline

her 'ear' for a good story.

© Hodder Children's Books 2006

Published in Great Britain in 2006
by Hodder Children's Books

Editor: Isabel Thurston
Design by Fiona Webb
Cover design: Hodder Children's Books

10 9 8 7 6 5 4 3 2 1

ISBN: 0 340 91186 7

Printed by Bookmarque Ltd, Croydon, Surrey

The paper and board used in this paperback by Hodder Children's Books are natural recyclable products made from wood grown in sustainable forests. The manufacturing processes conform to the environmental regulations of the country of origin.

Hodder Children's Books
a division of Hodder Headline Limited
338 Euston Road
London NW1 3BH

CONTENTS

INTRODUCTION

You've read the three books from cover to cover, maybe more than once, but how much do you really remember about *His Dark Materials*? This book contains over a thousand questions based on Philip Pullman's wonderful trilogy, and a sprinkling from the companion book, *Lyra's Oxford*. There's an Easy Quiz to get you started, 19 Medium Quizzes, and a Hard Quiz at the end to challenge you. So prepare to relive the extraordinary adventures of Lyra and Will, and find out how well you know *His Dark Materials*.

About the author

Clive Gifford is the author of more than 80 books for children and adults including *The Water Puppets*, *How To Live on Mars* and *Pants Attack*! He is the author of Hodder's *So You Think You Know* series of quiz books including titles on *The Simpsons*, *The Lord of the Rings*, *Roald Dahl*, *Narnia*, *Premier League Football* and *The Da Vinci Code*. Clive can be contacted at his website: www.clivegifford.co.uk.

EASY
QUESTIONS

1. What is the name of the young girl who is in all the books in the *His Dark Materials* trilogy?

2. Who is the author of the *His Dark Materials* series?

3. Is Serafina Pekkala a scholar, a witch or an angel?

4. What sort of creature is Iorek Byrnison?

5. In which of the books do we first meet Will?

6. What is the name of the creatures who form part of every human in Lyra's world?

7. Which two humans fall in love in *The Amber Spyglass*?

8. What relation does Lyra think Lord Asriel is to her at the start of *Northern Lights*?

9. What is the name of the English city in which the first book in the series opens?

10. In which book do we first meet Lord Asriel?

11. What vehicle does Lee Scoresby own?

12. According to Iorek Byrnison, do bears have ghosts or not?

13. Which of Will's hands is hurt badly in *The Subtle Knife*?

14. In what sort of portable home do the gyptian families live?

15. What is the name of the boy who is Lyra's best friend in *Northern Lights*?

16. Who offers first to live in the other's world: Will or Lyra?

17. From which continent does King Ogunwe hail?

18. Whose wound has improved greatly at the start of *The Amber Spyglass*?

19. What is the name of Lyra's dæmon?

20. After Iorek Byrnison re-forges the subtle knife, is it longer, shorter or much heavier?

21. According to the mulefa, is sraf their word for: evil, Dust or Lyra?

22.   Who turns out to be Lyra's mother?

23.   According to Ma Costa, is Lyra: a fire person,
      a water person or an earth person?

24.   In which book do we first meet Father
      MacPhail?

25.   What is the first name of the boy who searches
      for his father throughout *The Subtle Knife*?

26.   Roger lived in St Michael's College: true or
      false?

27.   What relation does Lord Asriel turn out to be
      to Lyra?

28.   In *Lyra's Oxford*, what colour is Sebastian
      Makepeace's cat dæmon?

29.   In which book does Lee Scoresby meet his
      death?

30.   In which city does Mrs Coulter live with Lyra?

31.   Will had three great friends back in Oxford:
      true or false?

32.   Which character has a snow leopard as their
      dæmon?

33. Is John Faa a scholar, a gyptian or a panserbørne?

34. Who does Lyra's dæmon once lick when they are wounded?

35. What three-lettered shortened name does Lyra often call her dæmon?

36. What is the first name of the bear that Lyra grows to love during her adventures?

37. In *The Amber Spyglass*, do dæmons follow their humans into the land of the dead?

38. Which lady do the mulefa ask to save their trees from sickness?

39. Which friend does Lyra meet in the land of the dead?

40. Which friend does Will have to think of to break the subtle knife for a second and final time?

41. In which city is Jordan College situated?

42. What ghostly creatures, beginning with the letter S, feed on the consciousness of adults?

43. What is the name of the Oxford college which is Lyra's home in *Northern Lights*?

44. What is the name of the haunted city where Will and Lyra meet: Oxford, Trollesund or Cittàgazze?

45. What is the name of the fortune-telling instrument that Lyra is given?

46. Is Mrs Coulter: married to Lord Asriel, a widow or married to Lord Boreal?

47. In which of the books do we first meet Serafina Pekkala?

48. What animal form do most servants' dæmons take?

49. What substance, beginning with the letter D, does Lord Asriel tell Lyra makes the alethiometer work?

50. Roger tells Lyra that he is more afraid of which Lord than he is of Mrs Coulter?

MEDIUM
QUESTIONS

1. In which city does Will lose two fingers of his hand?

2. In *Northern Lights*, is Lyra summoned to see the Master for the last time before her last dinner, last lunch or last breakfast at Jordan College?

3. Tony Makarios lived in Gabriel College: true or false?

4. Which woman is trying to get funds to keep the Dark Matter Research Unit open?

5. Whose ghost tells Will to cut Lyra's hair down to the scalp?

6. In *The Subtle Knife*, how much money does Will draw out of the cash dispenser in Summertown?

7. What does Will tell Balthamos is the main ingredient of Kendal Mint Cake?

8. Once Lee lets the last of his ballast go, in which one direction only can his balloon travel?

9. At the start of *The Amber Spyglass*, who is in a deep sleep?

10. What part of Will's body does he have to use to close a window onto another world?

11. Lyra had travelled all over the roof of Jordan College, except for: the Pilgrim's Tower, the Sheldon Building or the Great Hall?

12. Lyra travels with which family on the Grand Junction Canal in London?

13. What sort of creature does Will first kill with the subtle knife?

14. In *Northern Lights*, which two children visit Lord Asriel's house in Svalbard?

15. Can you name either of the gifts the mulefa give Mary as she leaves?

16. What seeds were always served after a feast at Jordan College?

17. Is Joachim Lorenz: a gyptian from *Northern Lights*, a horserider from *The Subtle Knife* or a Skraeling from *The Amber Spyglass*?

18. In *The Subtle Knife*, who is the only person who knows the ultimate purpose of the subtle knife?

19. Does Juta Kamainen have an osprey, a thrush, a robin or a pigeon for a dæmon?

20. How many cinemas do Lyra and Will go to on Lyra's first day in Will's Oxford?

21. Who arrives at the Experimental Station at Bolvangar by airship?

22. Who gives Lyra the potion to wake her up?

23. What does Serafina believe Æsahættr means: key of truth, the subtle knife, god-destroyer?

24. What sort of animal is Lee Scoresby's dæmon?

25. In *The Subtle Knife*, by what other name are the Watchers or *bene elim* known?

26. In *Northern Lights*, anbarology was a subject Lyra studied at school: true or false?

27. In *The Amber Spyglass*, who is the first person brought before the Consistorial Court of Discipline?

28. Is Xaphania male, female or of no sex?

29. How many zeppelin airships chase Lee Scoresby's balloon towards the end of *The Subtle Knife*?

30. When locked into her bedroom at the College of St Jerome, who does Mrs Coulter discover is in the room with her?

31. What is the name of the creature, beginning with the letter H, that meets Lyra, Will and the others at the gate to the land of the dead?

32. Had Will's father been in the Commandos, the Royal Air Force or the Royal Marines?

33. King Ogunwe reports to Lord Asriel that they killed how many Swiss Guards in capturing Mrs Coulter: 17, 32, 48 or 110?

34. Which one of the following is not a symbol on an alethiometer: a beehive, a skull, a church or an anchor?

35. Who carves a dæmon-coin for Tony Makarios and slips it into his mouth?

36. Who gave the alethiometer to Jordan College some years earlier?

37. Who stops Lyra from being separated from Pantalaimon in an operation at the Experimental Station?

38. Who is visited by a night-ghast at bedtime after playing around in the crypts earlier?

39. Who does Sir Charles Latrom tell that the subtle knife's other name translates as 'the last knife of all'?

40. What is the name of the tree that witches use for flying?

41. Will kills Juta Kamainen: true or false?

42. Who hid the baby Lyra in a closet when Mrs Coulter's husband arrived in Oxfordshire in a rage?

43. Before she became a scientist, what was Mary Malone?

44. Armoured bears in Svalbard are known by what name: night-ghasts, panserbørne or Gobblers?

45. In *The Amber Spyglass*, what nationality is Father MacPhail?

46. What object can be used to cut an opening into a different world?

47. Will vomits with horror shortly after he kills a member of which military force?

48. Who gives Lee Scoresby a flower from her crown which he can use to call for her help?

49. Who carries the Book of Changes with her as she travels through the Spectre-infected world?

50. What do Will and Lyra's dæmons tell them must be done to every single window into another world?

QUIZ 2

1. Is Mrs Coulter's hair dark, blond or silver?

2. After withdrawing money out of a bank machine, how much does Will give Lyra?

3. What colour is the poison powder the Master pours into the bottle of wine meant for Lord Asriel?

4. Who is the first ghost to step back out into the world of the living and vanish?

5. Martin Lanselius is a consul for which group: the witches, the bears or the Oblation Board?

6. In *The Amber Spyglass*, who spits in Lord Asriel's face?

7. When Lyra calls something anbaric, what word does Will use instead?

8. Which two new recruits to the gyptians' expedition had fought together before in the Tunguska campaign?

9. Was the name of the lawyer handling Will's father's affairs: Albert Jackson, Andrew Mayweather or Alan Perkins?

10. Do harpies see the best in everyone, the worst in everyone or learn each ghost's most important secret?

11. Can you name either the first or second rule regarding the subtle knife?

12. How many times had Mrs Coulter visited the College of St Jerome before her trip in *The Amber Spyglass*?

13. When offered a toy from a drawer at Bolvangar, does Lyra pick: a cuddly bear, a rag doll, a toy sword or a wooden horse?

14. In *Northern Lights*, can you name either of the characters that Lyra tells Lord Asriel she loves more than him?

15. What creatures feast on Father Gomez's body: cliff-ghasts, lizards, the mulefa or rats?

16. Which child is with Balthamos when he hears that Baruch is dead?

17. The Chevalier Tialys is a spy for Lord Asriel, a chief prosecutor of the Magisterium or the Lord Regent of the Authority?

18. Will uses a pot of ointment invented by whom, to help heal Lyra's head wound?

19. Can witches' dæmons travel greater or lesser distances away than humans' dæmons?

20. It is traditional for bears in combat to the death to rip out what part of their defeated opponent's body?

21. Umaq is the dog sledge driver hired by: Mrs Coulter, Lord Asriel, Iorek Byrnison or Lee Scoresby?

22. Where does Lyra lead Will and Mary Malone, when they are finally back in Will's Oxford?

23. What is the nickname, beginning with the letter C, of the computer in the Dark Matter Research Unit?

24. In his previous world, by what name had Stanislaus Grumman been known?

25. What was the name, beginning with the letter G, of the people whose children Lyra and the other college children viewed as their biggest enemies?

26. In *Lyra's Oxford*, what subject does the scholar Miss Greenwood specialize in: history, theology or alchemy?

27. What are the hundreds of black shapes Lyra and Iorek Byrnison see in the sky during their journey between Trollesund and the Station: crows, witches, Dust or night-ghasts?

28. In *Northern Lights*, who had all his property confiscated as the result of a lawsuit for killing a man?

29. Who was in the Parley Room with Farder Coram and Lyra?

30. Who asks Lord Asriel if they can go with him on his journey to the North and is told they cannot, but that Asriel will bring them back a walrus tusk?

31. What sort of food is Tony Makarios holding instead of his dæmon when Lyra finds him?

32. How many different rules about the subtle knife does Giacomo tell Will?

33. After Baruch dies, Lord Asriel orders a zeppelin tanker and a squadron of gyropters to take off. In what compass direction are the craft to head?

34. Who tells Lyra that a dæmon can only live fully in the world it was born in?

35. What item of his father's clothing does Will take after his father dies: his cloak, his hat, his boots or his knife belt?

36. In *Northern Lights*, Lord Asriel intends to make a bridge between the North and another world: true or false?

37. To which city was Lord Asriel heading the day after his meeting at Jordan College?

38. Is it a gross breach of etiquette to touch another person's dæmon: yes or no?

39. After she runs away in London, does the man with the top hat try to put a sleeping potion, some brandy or a poison into Lyra's coffee?

40. Who kills the witch tortured by Mrs Coulter on the ship to save her any more pain?

41. Serafina Pekkala won't land on the ground in Cittàgazze: because of an evil curse, because the ground is too mountainous or because of the Spectres?

42. Who came up with the idea of cutting people away from their dæmons?

43. What is the name, beginning with the letter T, of the elder brother of the two children, who was holding the subtle knife?

44. The police inspector tricks Lyra into mentioning that Will is with her: true or false?

45. What is the name of the queen of the Latvian witches?

46. At which London institute does Lyra spot Dr Broken Arrow and Colonel Carborn?

47. What does Mrs Coulter tell Lena Feldt she will do to Lyra?

48. How is Lord Boreal killed: with a knife, a gun, by a spell or by drinking poison?

49. What gruesome item did Lord Asriel store in a vacuum container before showing the scholars?

50. What water creature does Ma Costa cook for
    Lyra before they go to the Roping in the Fens?

QUIZ 3

1. How many hands does Lyra's alethiometer have?

2. When Lyra and Will first see the subtle knife, is it
   in the hands of Sir Charles, Tullio or Giacomo?

3. What becomes the name of Will's dæmon: Kalata,
   Kirjava or Kulang?

4. How many colleagues were with John Parry
   the first time he walked through a window into
   another world?

5. What figures are found on the handle of the
   subtle knife?

6. Who surprised Dr Malone when she returned to
   the Dark Matter Research Unit?

7. In *Northern Lights*, had Lord Asriel found the
   body of Stanislaus Grumman on ice off
   Trollesund, Bolvangar or Svalbard?

8. How many women are present at the Master's
   house, the first time Lyra meets Mrs Coulter?

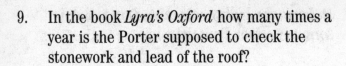

9. In the book *Lyra's Oxford* how many times a year is the Porter supposed to check the stonework and lead of the roof?

10. What does Iofur Raknison want more than anything: a dæmon, the throne of Svalbard or Mrs Coulter's hand in marriage?

11. Who tells Mrs Coulter that he stole the alethiometer?

12. What destroys the first zeppelin chasing Lee and Grumman?

13. Is Erik Andersson a painter, an explorer, a dancer or a balloonist?

14. In *Northern Lights*, which European city is the seat of the papacy: Rome, Geneva, Paris or Berlin?

15. Which two characters accompany Will when he finally sets off to return to his own world?

16. Is the tempter of Lyra to be a man, a woman, a bear or an angel?

17. What does Iorek Byrnison use to lubricate the panels of his armour?

18. In *Northern Lights*, whose dæmon is the first to seriously attack Pantalaimon?

19. Was Tony Makarios a gyptian enemy of Lyra's, a kitchen boy or a boy from Limehouse?

20. Ruud and Nellie Koopman were saved from the floods of '53 by which member of Lyra's family?

21. What name does 'John' translate into in Father Semyon's language: Boris, Jacques, Viktor or Ivan?

22. Is Sergeant Clifford a policeman, a policewoman or a member of Lord Asriel's army?

23. What is the name of Lord Asriel's first spy-captain?

24. Who tells the Consistorial Court of Discipline that Mrs Coulter has Lyra in her care in the Himalayas?

25. What sort of vehicle is waiting to take Lord Asriel from Jordan College to White Hall?

26. Which wheeled creatures are able to see Dust?

27. Which member of the force that heads to Bolvangar likes to play cards and smoke a cigar?

28. What creatures are Will and Lyra able to see for the first time after leaving the land of the dead?

29. What animal form does King Ogunwe's dæmon take?

30. Lee Scoresby's balloon cannot carry Iorek Byrnison: true or false?

31. Is Iorek's armour made of sky-iron, cloud-pine or battle-gold?

32. What sweet, sticky food does Will put on the tabby cat's injured ear to help it heal?

33. Are all harpies male, female or of no sex?

34. In *The Subtle Knife*, what does Lyra tell Will is the best thing she has ever seen?

35. Are the places at Jordan College's high table laid with platinum, silver or gold cutlery?

36. Which character in *The Subtle Knife* rejected the love of Juta Kamainen?

37. Mrs Coulter gives Lyra a drink at the Experimental Station. Is it a harmless camomile drink, a sleeping potion or a slow poison?

38. In *The Subtle Knife*, which of Lyra's allies spots Mrs Coulter on board a ship?

39. Can you name either of the colleges that stood beside Jordan College?

40. What is the name of the land where Lyra and Will believe the ghost of Roger is located?

41. Which character in *The Subtle Knife* was brought up as a Catholic: the Master, Serafina Pekkala or Mary Malone?

42. Who fights a battle to the death to allow Stanislaus Grumman to continue his quest to help the bearer of the subtle knife?

43. Is Lyra seasick or not in the early stages of her voyage with the gyptians to the North?

44. What is the name of the bar in Trollesund where Iorek Byrnison is given spirits to drink?

45. Which gyptian spy is badly wounded but manages to return to John Faa and the others?

46. Does John Faa say the last time his hammer drew blood was when he killed a Windsucker, a Tartar or a panserbørne?

47. In *Northern Lights*, who shows a human head to the Master and others, causing a stir?

48. Father MacPhail tells the rest of the Consistorial Court that they must destroy which organization that is studying Dust?

49. What object does Will cut to make a group of attacking children fall to the ground?

50. What name do the animals with round seed pods on their legs give themselves when Dr Malone tells them her name is Mary?

QUIZ 4

1. Who is the father of Serafina Pekkala's child?

2. In *Lyra's Oxford*, who does Lyra ask to look at the Oxford directory: Dr Polstead, the Porter or the Master?

3. What vehicles do Lord Faa and his force use to travel inland from the port towards Bolvangar?

4. In *Northern Lights*, which of the scholars says that Lyra will have to betray someone and it will hurt her greatly?

5. Do Iorek and Will first meet in Siberia, Svalbard or Trollesund?

6. Lyra's first lunch in London is at: the Savoy, the Royal Arctic Institute or the Waldorf?

7. What is the name of Dr Malone's male colleague in *The Subtle Knife*?

8. Bands of what metal are exchanged by mulefa couples when they get married?

9. What is the two word name given to the place where the Authority lives?

10. How are the children taken from Trollesund to the Experimental Station: by air, on foot or by sledge?

11. Lord Roke has a spy in the Society of the Work of the Holy Spirit. Is it Lord Grimal, Lady Salmakia or Dr Lanselius?

12. What was the name of the bill in Parliament which Lord Asriel defeated, to the benefit of the gyptians?

13. Which member of the gyptians' expedition do Samoyed hunters capture and take to Bolvangar?

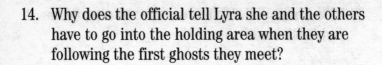

14. Why does the official tell Lyra she and the others have to go into the holding area when they are following the first ghosts they meet?

15. Does Lord Asriel give his lecture in the Hall, the Chapel or The Retiring Room of Jordan College?

16. Are the mulefa good swimmers, excellent sailors or do they never venture into the water?

17. Whose canal boat had Lyra hijacked in a battle with the gyptians in the past?

18. Which of the scholars was the Master's closest ally: the Chaplain, the Librarian, the Sub-Rector or the Cassington Scholar?

19. In *Northern Lights*, how many planets were thought to revolve around the Sun?

20. Who, near the end of *Northern Lights*, heads to Nova Zembla after he has fought off the cliff-ghasts?

21. Which one of these facts about Bernie Johansen is not true: he is a pastry cook, he kept watch over Lyra, he is of pure gyptian blood?

22. In which two seasons of the year did gyptian families come and go at the fairs?

23. Who buys Will a fine linen shirt to replace his bloodstained t-shirt?

24. In *Northern Lights*, who hopes to buy a farm and some cattle when he retires?

25. In *The Amber Spyglass*, which ill character disappears as an orderly opens the door in Lord Asriel's tower room?

26. Is Sir Charles Latrom's house in the Cowley, Jericho or Old Headington area of Oxford?

27. What word, beginning with the letter I, describes the separation of children from their dæmons?

28. What is the name of the angel who tells Lord Asriel about the subtle knife?

29. Who poisons himself shortly after saying goodbye to Will and Lyra?

30. In which city in Brytain had Jordan College bought an office block?

31. Who fashions two tins for Lyra while they are in the North?

32. Who uses the intention craft to rescue Mrs Coulter from the site of the Church's bomb launch?

33. What colour are Lyra's eyes?

34. Which girl from Cittàgazze does Father Gomez question about Dr Malone?

35. In the holding area, who warns Lyra not to call up her own death: Will, the Chevalier Tialys or Iorek?

36. In *The Subtle Knife*, who has never washed their hair themselves?

37. Mrs Lonsdale sends Lyra along to whose lodgings, where she meets Dame Hannah Relf?

38. Serafina tells Lyra that the oldest witch-mother is nearly: 600, 800, 1000 or 1200 years old?

39. Did Lyra originally think her mother and father died in New Denmark, Africa or the North?

40. Who volunteers to have their dæmon severed in order for the bomb to destroy Lyra to work?

41. Is Mr Cawson the Steward, the Butler or the Porter at Jordan College?

42. In which book does a witch's dæmon, in the form of a bird, try to lure Lyra and Pantalaimon into a trap?

43. Does Tony Makarios steal a pie, a sandwich or an apple from the market in Limehouse?

44. Can you name two of the three non-bears that Iorek tells Will he has a high regard for?

45. Who mapped the ocean currents of the Great Northern Ocean: Dr Wolf's Fang, Dr Broken Arrow or Dr Mended Heart?

46. A group of which warlike people guard the Station in the North?

47. Which two of the following items were in the area enclosed by a high wall behind the Tower of the Angels: fruit trees, beds of herbs, a fountain, a small temple, a large statue?

48. In *The Subtle Knife*, who brutally snaps and breaks one of the captured witch's fingers?

49. Which King changes his mind and agrees to let Mrs Coulter stay as Lord Asriel and others discuss military plans?

50. Sayan Kötör is the dæmon of which character: Stanislaus Grumman, Ruta Skadi, Ieva Kasku or Lord Boreal?

1. Who kills Father Gomez?

2. In which book does Lyra first leave her own world?

3. What is the name of the boy Lyra discovers in a village fish-house?

4. Ama's father is a herdsman of what animal?

5. Who tells Lyra that she must leave Jordan College: Mrs Lonsdale, the Intercessor or the Master?

6. Who does Metatron hit in the head with a rock as he is attacked in the Clouded Mountain?

7. What is Will's surname?

8. Which airship, the first, second or third, hunting for Lee and Grumman is destroyed by huge flocks of birds weighing it down so that it crashes?

9. What does Lyra throw against the window of Sir Charles Latrom's house to cause a distraction?

10. Does Lyra first meet Will in a café, a hotel on the beach or in a tower at Cittàgazze?

11. While searching for which friend does Lyra race up to the roof of Jordan College?

12. After quizzing the alethiometer, how many men does Lyra say are guarding the Experimental Station: 30, 60, 90 or 120?

13. Who cuts a piece of Iorek's armour into shreds using the subtle knife?

14. Who, apart from Lyra and Will, sees the ghosts arrive in the new world and then vanish?

15. What is the pattern on the skirt Lyra wears along with a green blouse from Cittàgazze?

16. In *Northern Lights*, is the Porter's name Cawson, Shuter or Grange?

17. What sort of boat takes Lyra, Will and the others to the land of the dead: a paddle steamer, a ghostly galleon, an old rowing boat or a raft made of giant trees?

18. Towards the end of *The Subtle Knife*, how long does the witch, Lena Feldt, take to make herself invisible before watching Mrs Coulter: an instant, ten minutes, 30 minutes or two hours?

19. Which character in *The Subtle Knife* is a shaman and had joined the Yenesi Pakhtars?

20. What animal symbol on the alethiometer means Africa?

21. Would the ghosts at the refugee camp town make their next journey by boat, by foot deep underground or by air?

22. What name is given to the children who lose their parents to Spectres?

23. Is the body of Tony Makarios buried, dropped into the sea or cremated?

24. Which one of the following is not a part of the magic potion created by the witches in *The Subtle Knife*: bloodmoss, spider-silk, oak bark, saltweed?

25. What is the name of the wine that Lord Asriel particularly likes: port, Madeira, Tokay or Massala?

26. Which angel is with Will when he first cuts windows into a whole series of different worlds?

27. Is the President of the Consistorial Court of Discipline called Father Gomez, Father MacPhail or Dr Cooper?

28. Does the goose-dæmon that Lyra spots in Trollesund belong to a witch, Mrs Coulter or a Tartar?

29. What new surname does Iorek give Lyra in recognition of her ability to tell tales?

30. What is the name of the old man who shares a cell in Svalbard with Lyra: Jotham Santelia, Marcus Rathbone or Geoffrey Trelawney?

31. Does Martha, Annie or Sister Clara say that when Mrs Coulter arrives at the Experimental Station, children tend to disappear?

32. Which allies of Lyra's does Serafina plan to visit after meeting with Iorek Byrnison?

33. When the gyptians approach Colby Water, Lyra is let out above decks for the first time in a while. What bird's form does Pantalaimon take?

34. Shadow-particles are the scientific name given to what substance first encountered in *Northern Lights*?

35. Which witch-queen in *The Subtle Knife* is keen to join forces with Lord Asriel and fight: Ruta Skadi, Reina Mita or Ieva Kasku?

36. In *Lyra's Oxford*, did the witch's dæmon learn to tell the time in Trollesund, Muscovy, Svalbard or Nova Zembla?

37. What word, beginning with the letter G, was the nickname given to the shady figures that were kidnapping children?

38. What two colours is the tent that Dr Malone finds and enters in Oxford?

39. Who killed Mrs Coulter's husband?

40. Animals and birds fled and no longer lived in the area around Bolvangar: true or false?

41. Who, in *Northern Lights*, has a sentry's head in their mouth and is stopped from crushing it by Lyra?

42. What is the colour of the house that the Witch-Consul in Trollesund lives in?

43. In *The Subtle Knife*, one of Lyra's allies kills a Skraeling: on Svalbard, Nova Zembla or in Cittàgazze?

44. Does Will, Lyra or Mrs Coulter first attempt to enter the Tower of the Angels?

45. Every time a window is made with the subtle knife, what creature is created?

46. What type of animal do the scholars mean when they refer to panserbørne?

47. What is the occupation of the woman Will leaves his mother with?

48. Gallivespians are much smaller than regular humans, much taller than regular humans or about the same size?

49. When Iorek Byrnison and Lyra are reunited in *The Amber Spyglass*, can you name two of the three other characters who settle round the fire to share food?

50. What colour eyes does Serafina Pekkala have?

QUIZ 6

1. Who lures Tony Makarios into a London warehouse where there are other children?

2. Which one of the following items does Will not take from the campsite containing the dead body of Lord Boreal: fish hooks, a first-aid kit, a revolver, a magnifying glass?

3. Which animal's liver does Mrs Coulter tell Lyra is full of poison and will kill you in minutes?

4. What name, beginning with the letter C, is the big-eyed lizard symbol on Lyra's alethiometer?

5.   What started to happen to the frozen lands where Iorek lived, once Lord Asriel made the bridge between different worlds?

6.   What natural object are Will and Lyra following when Father Gomez trains his rifle sights on them?

7.   Who is attacked by Spectres shortly after losing a fight with Will?

8.   How old is Ama at the start of *The Amber Spyglass*?

9.   In *The Subtle Knife*, the alethiometer tells Lyra to concern herself with finding what relation of Will's?

10. The arrival of two Gallivespians allows which character to grab Mrs Coulter's pistol?

11. Mrs Lonsdale is related to Lyra, Lord Asriel, Roger or the Master?

12. Who does Iorek fence with to prove that bears cannot be tricked?

13. In *The Amber Spyglass*, Iorek has chartered a ship to sail in which compass direction?

14. Who names Will's dæmon?

15. Who buys a gas engined boat and heads up river to find Stanislaus Grumman?

16. The Society of the Work of the Holy Spirit believes that who is the most important child that has ever lived?

17. Was Lyra on a gyptian narrow boat, in London with Mrs Coulter, or sailing on the German Ocean when she first encountered a spy-fly?

18. The boatman who will take the travellers to the land of the dead, refuses to take one of the party. Is it Will, Pantalaimon, the Chevalier Tialys or Lyra?

19. Trepanning involves cutting a hole in what part of the body?

20. Who kills Will's father: Juta Kamainen, Serafina Pekkala or Lee Scoresby?

21. The philosophers in Cittàgazze pass into other worlds: to fight wars, to help those in need or to steal?

22. How many legs does the intention craft have?

23. Is Dr Broken Arrow a Skraeling, a Lascar or a Tartar?

24. Who puts their passport photo on a library card to fool the police: Will, Mrs Coulter or Mary Malone?

25. When being chased by balloons in *The Subtle Knife*, does Lee Scoresby want to head for Cittàgazze, the fortress at Svalbard or a range of hills?

26. On what vehicle do Lord Roke, Mrs Coulter and others head into Lord Asriel's armoury?

27. Who visits the great healer, Pagdzin *tulku*, at the monastery at Cho-Lung-Se?

28. The Consistorial Court of Discipline is made up of eight, ten or twelve members?

29. What does Lyra tell people at Mrs Coulter's cocktail party is her father's title: Lord, Bishop or Count?

30. What was the richest college in Oxford: Jordan, Gabriel or St Martin's?

31. Who eats the body of Lee Scoresby?

32. In what vehicle do the gyptians say the Gobblers came: a horse-drawn wagon, a steam train or a truck?

33. What type of insect do the Gallivespians breed and use for transport?

34. Which of the Jordan College scholars had made several trips to the Arctic: the Cassington Scholar, the Sub-Rector or the Palmerian Professor?

35. Which one of the following is not present when Lord Asriel shows the slides of his expedition to the North: the Sub-Enquirer, the Chaplain or the Cassington Scholar?

36. Does Dr Malone store the new program for the Cave computer on a compact disc, a floppy disk, a pen drive or a laptop computer?

37. In *The Amber Spyglass*, have Iorek Byrnison and the other bears stolen their ship, built it themselves or hired it by paying in gold?

38. Can you name either of the men to whom Lyra first shows the alethiometer?

39. Who becomes the official bearer of the knife after Giacomo Paradisi?

40. Does the first bullet that touches Lee Scoresby graze his arm, thigh or scalp?

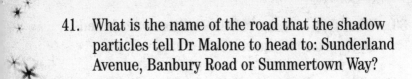

41. What is the name of the road that the shadow
    particles tell Dr Malone to head to: Sunderland
    Avenue, Banbury Road or Summertown Way?

42. What kind of stone was Iofur Raknison's throne
    made of: marble, granite or shale?

43. Lee Scoresby shoots the Skraeling in what part
    of his body?

44. The Muscovy army's engine, which can burn
    down a wet forest, was developed for fighting:
    Nippon, Norroway or New Denmark?

45. In *Lyra's Oxford*, is Michael Coke a well-known:
    flautist, alchemist, physicist or thief?

46. Clarice Walk in London is the home of
    Mrs Coulter, Tony Makarios or Lord Asriel?

47. In which book do we first meet Dr Lanselius?

48. Does the oldest cliff-ghast say Lord Asriel's
    army will fail without: Lyra, the alethiometer
    or Æsahættr?

49. Which of the witches in *The Subtle Knife* has
    a dæmon called Sergei: Ruta Skadi, Juta
    Kamainen or Serafina Pekkala?

50. What small creature does Pantalaimon become to get closer to the alethiometer when he and Lyra first view it?

QUIZ 7

1. Which gyptian seals the spy-fly in an old smoke-leaf tin?

2. Who does Lyra cling to in pain as she leaves Pantalaimon on the shore?

3. What animal does Will first see disappear through the window into another world?

4. Who tells Lyra that Mrs Coulter lost her husband in an accident a few years ago?

5. Jacob Huismans is severely injured by what weapon: a musket, a sword or an arrow?

6. According to Tony Costa, who are half-killed warriors: Nälkäinens, Windsuckers or The Breathless Ones?

7. When Lyra sees the Zaal, is she at a meeting of gyptians, in the fortress at Svalbard or in Oxford with Will?

8. Who gives Ama a cure for sleeping sickness:
    Serafina Pekkala, Pagdzin *tulku* or Stanislaus
    Grumman?

9. Who asks Mr Basilides to pinpoint the location
    of the cave containing Lyra?

10. In *The Subtle Knife*, Sir Charles Latrom
    frequently wears: a bowler, a panama or a
    top hat?

11. There are five people at the observatory run by
    the Imperial Muscovite Academy. Are any of
    them Polish?

12. Which symbol does Lyra tell Farder Coram is for
    cunning?

13. Who grabs Father Gomez's dæmon just before
    he is going to shoot Lyra?

14. Can you name either of the two angels who
    accompany Will at the start of *The Amber
    Spyglass*?

15. Who was the first member of the gyptians'
    expedition to meet Lee Scoresby?

16. The brick-burners' children lived at Yarnton,
    by Gabriel College or by the Claybeds?

17. What does Ma Costa give Lyra to drink after she
     has been rescued by the gyptians from the men
     with nets?

18. What sort of tool is Mary Malone's most precious
     possession while she is in the land of the
     mulefa?

19. What is the name of the place where Lyra is
     reunited with Roger?

20. As they escape the cave, do the two Gallivespian
     spies tell Will and Lyra to head to: the Swiss
     Guard, the Africans or the open window into
     another world?

21. Lee Scoresby uses the Skraeling's ring to trick
     soldiers into giving him: a rifle, his balloon, the
     subtle knife or a key into the observatory?

22. Who had a palace built in the North made of
     imported marble: Iofur Raknison, Mrs Coulter,
     Serafina Pekkala or Iorek Byrnison?

23. What part of Mary's body are the mulefa most
     fascinated by?

24. When Will falls asleep while the witches prepare
     a healing spell, what natural object do the
     witches pile upon him to keep him warm?

25. In *Northern Lights*, does the King hold his weekly Council of State in Limehouse, White Hall or Falkeshall?

26. Can you name the second meaning of the hourglass symbol, according to Farder Coram?

27. Is Michael Canzona, Raymond van Gerrit or Adam Stefanski in charge of arms and weapons for the gyptians' expedition to the North?

28. The Sysselman is: the priest, governor or bar owner of Trollesund?

29. Were there ten, twelve or fourteen seats found at the High Table in Jordan College?

30. Do the people of Ama's village think Mrs Coulter is a bandit, a holy woman or the devil?

31. Who does Lyra try to act like when faced with a fight with a witch in the book, *Lyra's Oxford*?

32. Who does John Faa make treasurer for the expedition heading to the North: Roger van Poppel, Adam Stefanski or Simon Hartmann?

33. Was Mrs Coulter's husband: a senior politician, a senior figure in the Church or a scholar in Oxford?

34. What spiky creature does Pantalaimon turn
    into to ward off Mrs Coulter's dæmon as Ama
    watches?

35. Who comes up with the plan to let the ghosts
    escape from the land of the dead?

36. What sort of meal is served to Lyra and Will in
    the holding area as they search for the land of
    the dead: stew, salad, sandwiches or cold meat?

37. At the start of *The Subtle Knife*, does Will pack
    his things in: his school satchel, a rucksack, an
    old shopping bag or a battered leather suitcase?

38. Who wears a heavy gold chain and holds a
    pretend dæmon in the form of a stuffed doll,
    the first time Lyra meets him?

39. What is the best way of starting a fire, according
    to Stanislaus Grumman?

40. What creature does the Chevalier Tialys attempt
    to kill before dying himself?

41. Is the name of the witch who goes to spy on
    Mrs Coulter at the end of *The Subtle Knife*:
    Ruta Skadi, Lena Feldt or Juta Kamainen?

42. Can you name either the third or fourth rule
    regarding the subtle knife?

43. Which of Lyra's friends hits Will hard enough to make him fall over in *The Amber Spyglass*?

44. What is the name of Will's former piano teacher?

45. Is Captain Magnusson employed by John Faa and the gyptians, the bears of Svalbard or Mrs Coulter?

46. After the visit from Lord Asriel, which part of Jordan College does Lyra start exploring: the rooftops, the University Library or the underground vaults?

47. What is the first lesson activity Lyra does at the Experimental Station: gym class, theology, sewing or mathematics?

48. Who tells Will and Lyra that just one window between the worlds can be left open: Xaphania, Mary Malone, Lord Asriel or Serafina Pekkala?

49. Which bear did Mrs Coulter promise could be baptized as a Christian?

50. To which European city does Mrs Coulter travel in order to visit the College of St Jerome?

QUIZ 8

1. What animal does Will have as a pet at the start of *The Subtle Knife*?

2. Lee Scoresby and John Parry lead other ghosts out to fight which creatures?

3. Who is the first human Will and Lyra meet after leaving the great battle and entering a new world?

4. What does Iorek Byrnison ask to be returned to him as the price for his coming on the gyptians' expedition?

5. Whose dæmon leads the huge flocks of birds to destroy one of the airships hunting for Lee Scoresby's balloon?

6. What does Lee Scoresby aim for and hit with his very last bullet?

7. How many of Lyra's gold coins does she have to part with for some bread, cheese and fruit to share with Will as they travel through the countryside towards the end of *The Subtle Knife*?

8. In *The Subtle Knife*, which of the witches flies with the angels to Lord Asriel's fortress?

9. Is the first meaning of the anchor symbol on the alethiometer: hope, sea, faith or stubbornness?

45

10. What is the name of the female who becomes a good friend of Mary Malone's while she is with the mulefa?

11. The captured spy-fly is not black as Lyra first thought. What colour is it?

12. A harpy has the face and breasts of a woman but the body of which creature?

13. By what name, beginning with the letter Z, are the mulefa known individually?

14. Which member of the Costa family saves Lyra from the men with the nets in London?

15. In *Northern Lights*, how does Lyra originally say her mother and father died?

16. After the river boat has dropped all the bears off, do Iorek and Will continue on foot, hire a horse and cart or travel in Lee Scoresby's balloon?

17. Lord Asriel unties Mrs Coulter in his tower, but what creature is left in chains?

18. Lord Roke spies on three adults performing an experiment on a lock of Lyra's hair. Can you name two of them?

19. At the top of which number staircase did Lyra
     have her bedroom in Jordan College?

20. Who is unsure whether to repair the subtle knife
     and explains to Will that every tool has its own
     intentions?

21. Which one of the following is not a child
     prisoner at the Experimental Station: Bella,
     Joyce, Martha or Annie?

22. Which member of Mrs Coulter's staff at
     Bolvangar does Father MacPhail interrogate: Dr
     Johnson, Dr Rawforth, Dr Grissom or Dr Cooper?

23. In *Lyra's Oxford*, what type of white bird crashes
     into the witch before it can attack Lyra?

24. What is the name of the only weapon that can
     defeat The Authority?

25. Is Serafina Pekkala over 200, over 300, over 500
     or over 700 years old?

26. What item of his mother's does Lee Scoresby lay
     on the rock beside him as he fights to the death?

27. Who tells Mrs Coulter that the subtle knife is
     also known as Æsahættr?

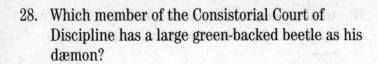

28. Which member of the Consistorial Court of Discipline has a large green-backed beetle as his dæmon?

29. Which gyptian boy does Lyra meet at lunchtime at the windowless canteen of the Experimental Station?

30. How many bears lived and worked in Trollesund?

31. What weapon is Father Gomez carrying as he enters the village of the mulefa where Will, Lyra and Mary are staying?

32. Who returns the envelope containing most of Lyra's hair to Mrs Coulter?

33. In *Northern Lights*, an underground railway in London is called an Anbaric, a Naphta or a Chthonic Railway?

34. In which building does Sir Charles Latrom say the subtle knife is hidden?

35. How long in inches was the original blade of the subtle knife: three, five, eight or ten?

36. Black Shuck is the name of: a ghost dog, a deep lake in Svalbard or a giant mountain in the North?

37. In *The Subtle Knife*, which dæmon breaks etiquette to touch a person who isn't their own human?

38. On what subject is the book at the bottom of Mary Malone's rucksack?

39. In *Northern Lights*, does John Faa, Lord Asriel or the Witch-Consul ask Lyra to use the alethiometer to find out about the Tartars?

40. What creature sucks the life out of the witch, Lena Feldt?

41. Which character in the *His Dark Materials* series has the surname Belacqua?

42. At the Experimental Station what do the children decide will be the signal to start their escape?

43. What is the name of the angel, beginning with the letter M, who some other angels call Lord Regent?

44. Whose dæmon holds Roger's dæmon in her mouth, to Lyra's horror?

45. Which one of the following was not in the bag Will packed to leave home: deodorant, toothpaste, chocolate bars, his mother's purse?

46. At the dinner at the Master's house, Mrs Coulter says she met Lord Asriel at what scientific institute?

47. What beautiful-looking creature is Farder Coram's dæmon?

48. Does Lord Boreal have a serpent, a wolf or an eagle for his dæmon?

49. In *The Amber Spyglass*, who does Will insist on finding before going to see Lord Asriel?

50. In *Lyra's Oxford*, Yelena Pazhets is a scholar, a pupil at St Sophia's, a witch or a Cardinal?

QUIZ 9

1. The goose-dæmon tells Lyra that which gyptian was wounded in the attack when Lyra was kidnapped?

2. Does Lyra tell Lord Asriel that she knows he is her father in Cittàgazze, Jordan College or Svalbard?

3. What object is on the top of the hourglass symbol on Lyra's alethiometer?

4. Do the Stefanski family pledge 23, 38, 45 or 57 men to the gyptian expedition to the North?

5. Is Pagdzin *tulku*: an angel, a healer, a warlord or a witch?

6. Had Thorold been Lord Asriel's servant for almost 30, 40, 50 or 60 years?

7. What symbol, beginning with the letter M, represents Mrs Coulter on Lyra's alethiometer?

8. Who surprises Will and Lyra's dæmons just as they are coming back to Will and Lyra in the mulefa village?

9. How many crossbow bolts could a Swiss Guard load and fire a minute: five, ten or fifteen?

10. Which angel first goes through into Lyra's world to try and find her?

11. Falkeshall Gardens is: the landing place for the gyptians' narrow-boat, the zeppelin from Oxford or the ship bound for Trollesund?

12. Who sits on an old tree trunk in the land of the dead and tells stories of the living world to lots of ghosts?

13. Which place, after Burger King, does Will go to hide shortly after the man is killed in his house?

14. Whose loyal dæmon is called Hester?

15. Who makes the amber spyglass: Mary Malone, Lyra, Lord Asriel or the mulefa?

16. Pantalaimon is so upset at Lyra switching dæmon-coins in the skulls that he turns into: a rat, a bat or a wildcat?

17. What object used by Dr Malone does Lyra describe as an engine with words?

18. What is the only one object the Spectres are afraid of?

19. Lyra tells Iofur Raknison that she is a dæmon, but whose dæmon does she say she is?

20. Does Mrs Coulter eject a cardinal, a gyptian or a journalist from her cocktail party?

21. What gas can Lee Scoresby make from iron filings and acid to fill his hot-air balloon?

22. Is Fra Pavel's dæmon in the form of an eagle, a snake, a frog or a badger?

23. Who summons powers to down three out of four attacking zeppelins?

24. At Mrs Coulter's cocktail party, which Lord does Lyra tell that Roger was taken by the Oblation Board?

25. Do the oldest buildings of Jordan College stand around: Palmer's Quad, Meurer's Quad or Yaxley Quad?

26. Is the first name of the Librarian of Jordan College: Edgar, Charles or Jeremiah?

27. After which character in *Northern Lights* is Iofur Raknison planning to name his capital city?

28. Who owns the leather writing case Will tries to find in his house?

29. What sort of vehicles, powered by gas engines, patrol the skies searching for Lyra?

30. Lyra tells Mrs Coulter that she hopes in the future to capture a gyptian narrow-boat and sail it to: Teddington, Abingdon or Paddington?

31. When Will cuts a window into Lord Asriel's republic, are they in the middle of a prison, a forest, a battle or a giant pit?

32. What is the name of the housekeeper at Jordan College who calls Lyra down from the roof and helps wash and dress her?

33. In which European city does Dr Oliver Payne take a new job away from Oxford: Paris, Berlin, Hamburg or Geneva?

34. Is Nicholas Rokeby, Roger Baird or Jeremy Scarforth a head of one of the gyptian families?

35. Who is the first character to enter a world with giant trees and animals with diamond-shaped forms?

36. Who does Lyra tell that her parents were the Duke and Duchess of Abingdon: the Gallivespian spies, the harpy or the boatman taking them to the land of the dead?

37. What part of Iofur's body does Iorek remove with just one swipe of his paw?

38. What alternative name for the Experimental Station means fields of evil?

39. What substance does the Magisterium think is physical evidence of original sin?

40. Were gyropters, airships or witches used as a decoy for the intention craft?

41. Do Will and Iorek hear the zeppelins for the first time before or after Will has visited Mrs Coulter at the cave?

42. When Lyra first meets Will what surname does she give?

43. Juta Kamainen is a young witch. Is she just over 50, 100, 200 or 300 years old?

44. Who suggests to Dr Mary Malone that she could alter the computer in the Dark Matter Research Unit to print words instead of patterns?

45. The first time Lyra uses the alethiometer to ask about Will, what does she learn about him?

46. When Will first touches his own dæmon, what animal form is it in?

47. Can you name the two friends who travel in Lee Scoresby's balloon along with Lyra as they escape from Bolvangar?

48. The ghosts of which two adult allies do Lyra and Will meet in the land of the dead?

49. To the nearest two years, how many years do Gallivespians tend to live?

50. Who does John Faa put in charge of food and clothing stores: Roger van Poppel, Simon Hartmann or Adam Stefanski?

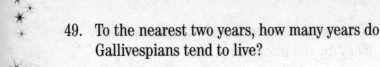

QUIZ 10

1. The River Isis flows through which town or city in *Northern Lights*?

2. What item does Sir Charles Latrom place in a locked glass cabinet in full view of Lyra and Will?

3. Who says that dæmons lead to troubling thoughts, which help let Dust in?

4. In *The Subtle Knife*, who does the Witch-Consul suggest Serafina Pekkala should visit to find out more about Lord Asriel?

5. Who is to be the tempter of Lyra?

6. What alcoholic fruit drink does Giacomo give Will after Will is injured?

7. How many quadrangles are the buildings of Jordan College grouped around?

8. What form does Sir Charles Latrom's dæmon take?

9. How many zeppelins does the Consistorial Court send to find Lyra?

10. According to Ma Costa, who had a gun the night Lord Asriel killed Mrs Coulter's husband?

11. Does Ma Costa live in a caravan, a hostel or a canal boat?

12. Does Jotham Santelia tell Lyra that he was invited by Iorek Byrnison, Lord Asriel or Iofur Raknison to be vice-chancellor of a university in Svalbard?

13. What false name does Lyra give to her kidnappers on the way to the Station in the North?

14. Lord Asriel orders Chevalier Tialys and Lady Salmakia to follow and help which male character?

15. Does Jacob Huismans die, disappear or recover from an injury?

16. What sweet food item does Will give Balthamos near the start of *The Amber Spyglass*?

17. Which of Lord Roke's spies breeds red and yellow striped dragonflies?

18. In *The Amber Spyglass*, what sort of creature is No-Name: a mulefa, a Gallivespian or a harpy?

19. Which friend of Lyra's is asked to join the witches' council by Serafina Pekkala?

20. Who is Lyra reunited with at the Experimental Station: Lord Asriel, Tony Makarios or Roger?

21. How old is Will at the start of *The Subtle Knife*?

22. Farder Coram says he had last seen a spy-fly in which North African country?

23. What is the name of the Cardinal who Serafina Pekkala kills with an arrow, in *The Subtle Knife*?

24. Mary Malone sees which character get off the back of a tualapi bird and enter the mulefa village?

25. In a compartment of which device in his house does Will find the leather writing case?

26. Whose dragonfly dies first in the land of the dead?

27. According to Thorold, what is the one thing Lord Asriel needs to complete his experiment to form a bridge into another world?

28. Intercision is the word used to describe the separation of a child from what?

29. What sort of metal made the wires that joined the plates of Iofur Raknison's armour?

30. Allan is the name of whose chauffeur?

31. What word, beginning with the letter R, does Lyra use to describe the Northern Lights to John Faa and Farder Coram?

32. Is Semyon Borisovitch: a male witch, a mercenary, a priest or a sergeant in the Imperial Muscovy Guard?

33. Where does Ama see Mrs Coulter put the lock of hair she cut from Lyra's head?

34. What is the full official name of the board nicknamed the Gobblers?

35. What final form does Lyra's dæmon take?

36. Who is the second human to enter the world of the mulefa, after Mary Malone?

37. When Will returns to the camp after meeting his father, which friend of his is missing?

38. What type of bird was ordered occasionally by the Bursar for a feast at Jordan College: eagle, ostrich or swan?

39. Who was placed in a Priory with the Sisters of Obedience as an infant?

40. What final form does Will's dæmon take?

41. Did Jerry, Captain Rokeby or Tony Costa have a dæmon in the form of a seagull?

42. What weapon does Metatron almost launch at Will the first time they meet?

43. Jericho is the setting for the Horse Fair in *Northern Lights*; in which city is Jericho?

44. What creature helps Lyra and others open the door to the building that turns out to contain severed dæmons?

45. Which of Adam's sons does Metatron say he is related to: Cain, Abel or Seth?

46. Which one of the following is not another name for The Authority: the Creator, Yahweh, the Prescient or Adonai?

47. Who fights his own father in *The Subtle Knife*?

48. Is Farder Coram, a gyptian, a panserbørne or a member of the Oblation Board?

49. Does Mrs Coulter, the Skraeling or Dr Grumman call Lee Scoresby an enemy of the church?

50. Had the Steward, the Porter or the Cook twice beaten Lyra in the past?

QUIZ 11

1. In *Lyra's Oxford*, Yelena Pazhets puts a drug in Sebastian Makepeace's: tea, wine, cocoa or medicine?

2. Who breaks his left leg trying to stop Father MacPhail's bomb from working?

3. Who does Father Semyon tell that armoured bears in a boat are nearby?

4. The Dark Matter Research Unit is first found in which book?

5. Does the Consistorial Court of Discipline hear evidence at The College of St Jerome, St Sophia's or St George's during *The Amber Spyglass*?

6. After regaining his armour, does Iorek head for the governor's house, the mountains or the harbour?

7. Who finally regains their courage for a moment to stand between Will and three members of the Swiss Guard?

8. Do the Church's forces travel by land, sea or air to find Lyra?

9. Does Ma Costa tell Lyra that gyptians are fire people, water people or earth people?

10. What is the name of the Board Mrs Coulter is the head of?

11. Which of the following do the gyptians present to the mulefa: a leather cloak, walrus ivory carvings, silver cups, a golden spear?

12. What happens to Lyra straight after she has gone through the window to Will's world for the first time?

13. When Will had once fought a boy who upset his mother, what part of the boy's body did he break?

14. How many winding wheels are there on Lyra's alethiometer?

15. In *Northern Lights*, what is unusual about Bernie Johansen's dæmon?

16. Does Lord Asriel blame: the Steward, the Butler or the Porter for smashing the decanter full of wine?

17. How many electrodes are put on Lyra's head by Dr Malone to allow her to communicate with the shadow-particles?

18. What word, beginning with the letter L, do gyptians use for people who are non-gyptians?

19. Is Belisaria the name of John Faa's, Jerry's or Mrs Coulter's dæmon?

20. Who tells the witches' prophecy about Lyra to Mrs Coulter?

21. Which ministry are Benjamin de Ruyter and the other spies breaking into when they are attacked?

22. What part of his armour does Iorek throw down in the challenge to Will in Siberia?

23. Is Grumman, Lee Scoresby or John Faa a Tartar by adoption?

24. In *The Amber Spyglass*, which valley is close to where the sleeping Lyra is located: the valley of thunder, valley of the rainbows or valley of eternal flowers?

25. Which two of the following has Lyra never encountered before meeting Will: chewing gum, stew, baked beans, gas lights?

26. Who returns to the Dark Matter Research Unit just before midnight?

27. In *Lyra's Oxford*, the witch who seeks to kill Lyra had had a son with: Dr Polstead, the Porter or Sebastian Makepeace?

28. What weapon does Mrs Coulter use to keep Will at bay in the cave?

29. Which gyptian saved a witch's life over 40 years ago?

30. Who spied Mrs Coulter forcing Lyra to drink a sleeping potion?

31. What make of motor vehicle is Sir Charles Latrom driven around in?

32. At the start of *Northern Lights*, which room in Jordan College does Lyra see for the first time?

33. What are the first creatures Will and Lyra meet after leaving the great battle, recovering their dæmons and entering a new world?

34. Who hurts Mrs Coulter with a spur tipped with poison?

35. Which church figure has a crow for a dæmon: Father Gomez, Father MacPhail or Father Semyon?

36. A Roping is a gathering of the Oblation Board, armoured bears or gyptians?

37. What sort of bird is Stanislaus Grumman's dæmon?

38. Who throws the first snowball during the fire drill at the Experimental Station?

39. In *Lyra's Oxford*, does Sebastian Makepeace live in Cowley, Headington or Jericho?

40. Which American state had Will's father been located in the last time he wrote a letter to Will's mother?

41. Who plans to set up a permanent inquisition in every world?

42. Who tells Lyra that her father is Lord Asriel?

43. Jimson weed ointment is used to: heal wounds, protect against insects or ward off Spectres?

44. Which gyptian asks Lyra to use the alethiometer to see what Mrs Coulter was doing?

45. In *Lyra's Oxford*, what subject is it said that Sebastian Makepeace studies: theology, alchemy, geography or physics?

46. Annie, a girl at Bolvangar, has a dæmon called Kyrillion. What animal form does it take: a fox, a goose, a polecat or a gerbil?

47. Tony Costa tells Lyra that Tartars bake and eat what type of person?

48. Whose dæmon takes the form of a golden monkey?

49. The dæmon whose name is Stelmaria takes the form of what animal?

50. Which new recruit to the gyptians' expedition insists on playing a card game called Hazard with some of the gyptians?

QUIZ 12

1. What is the first name of Will Parry's father?

2. Who do the two angels with Will at the start of *The Amber Spyglass* want him to see?

3. During his lecture at Jordan College, which king does Lord Asriel say that he set out on a diplomatic mission to meet?

4. Is Inspector Walters from Oxfordshire Police, the Fraud Squad or Special Branch?

5. What plant provides the tube for the amber spyglass?

6. In *Lyra's Oxford*, what is the name of the man the witch's dæmon is searching for?

7. After running away from Mrs Coulter's apartment, what is the first drink Lyra has?

8. What is the name of the witch who kills Will's father?

9. Who gives Lyra the alethiometer?

10. What creature does Iorek Byrnison capture and eat just before hearing of Lee Scoresby's death?

11. Metatron was the son of Jared, Abraham or Mahalalel?

12. Which musical instrument, beginning with the letter L, was a symbol on the alethiometer?

13. At the Experimental Station, what cooking ingredient does Lyra fill the kitchen with, hoping to create an explosion?

14. Were the mulefa attacked by tiger-like creatures, humans or giant birds?

15. From what country, in our world a US state, did Lee Scoresby come?

16. Where does Sir Charles place the key to the cabinet holding the alethiometer: in a desk drawer, in his safe or in his waistcoat pocket?

17. Are there 12, 24, 36 or 48 symbols on an alethiometer?

18. In what mountain range does Baruch tell Will that Lyra is located?

19. In the book *Lyra's Oxford*, who grabs the witch's dæmon and then falls through the trapdoor on the roof?

20. Whose death scratches his head then advises Will and the others to go to the jetty in order to be guided into the land of the dead?

21. At a museum in Will's Oxford, what object does Lyra's alethiometer date as 33,254 years old?

22. What colour is the hawk that Lord Roke rides like humans ride a horse?

23. What part of Grumman's body is very diseased: his liver, his lungs, his heart or his brain?

24. Can you name the witch queen other than Serafina Pekkala who flies into the new world with the other witches?

25. How long in inches are Iofur Raknison's claws?

26. All witches are on the side of Lyra and the gyptians in *Northern Lights*: true or false?

27. Can you give any of the other names by which the character Jopari is known?

28. With whom does Lyra get drunk in the wine cellars of Jordan College?

29. What sort of practice drill at the Experimental Station enables Lyra, Roger and Billy to explore outside the Experimental Station?

30. What does Mrs Coulter do with all the letters written by the kidnapped children to their parents?

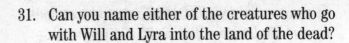

31. Can you name either of the creatures who go with Will and Lyra into the land of the dead?

32. Which wise gyptian man does it turn out has been keeping an eye out for Lyra throughout almost all of her life?

33. In *Lyra's Oxford*, a witch runs out of the house in Juxon Street carrying what weapon?

34. Who does Lyra rescue in *Northern Lights*, only for him to die while she sleeps?

35. Which spy of Lord Asriel's accompanies the intention craft when it is stolen?

36. On entering the Retiring Room for the very first time, does Lyra sit on a green leather armchair, the Master's throne or a dusty wooden bench?

37. Bella is one of the girls Lyra meets at the Experimental Station: true or false?

38. What answer do the shadow particles give to Dr Malone when she asks if they are the same as Lyra's Dust?

39. As the gyptians travel to Svalbard, what is the name of the reigning bear king?

40. Members of which force are carried by zeppelins to capture Lyra and Will?

41. Is Dr Payne or Dr Malone more interested in Sir Charles Latrom's offer of funding for the Dark Matter Research Unit?

42. What is the first thing Lyra spies Lord Asriel drinking in Jordan College?

43. When Balthamos first pretends to be Will's dæmon in front of other people, what sort of animal does he become?

44. Who is chased by cliff-ghasts as she returns to Serafina Pekkala and the other witches?

45. When Will and Lyra make their first trip back to Cittàgazze, they find a large number of children crowded around what animal?

46. Who is the last person Lyra says goodbye to as she escapes from Bolvangar in the hot-air balloon?

47. What is the first name of Will's mother?

48. Lyra shouts when she sees the poisoned wine about to be poured. Who does she alert with her cry?

49. Is Will dressing his wound, practising with the subtle knife or reading his father's letters when Lyra returns from his world after being chased by the police?

50. What precious item of Lyra's is left behind when she disappears at the end of *The Subtle Knife*?

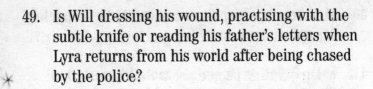

QUIZ 13

1. What does Iorek say he will do to the palace at Svalbard if he wins his combat with Iofur?

2. Which college is Hugh Lovat from: Gabriel, Jordan or St Michael's?

3. In what object does Lyra hide just before the Steward enters the Retiring Room?

4. Can you name either of the characters who use spider-silk reins and a hummingbird skin saddle to ride dragonflies away from the Church's airships?

5. Is Tony Makarios six, nine or eleven years old at the time he is captured by the Gobblers?

6. What is the first name, beginning with the letter M, of Mrs Coulter?

7.   In *Northern Lights*, Serafina Pekkala had a child who died 40 years earlier. Was it a boy or a girl?

8.   When quizzing people about Stanislaus Grumman, what explanation does Lee Scoresby give for his interest: he is owed money, Grumman is his brother or he wants to kill Grumman?

9.   After learning about the bomb in the College of St Jerome, who is the first person Lord Roke attacks with his poisoned spurs?

10. Lee Scoresby's balloon and equipment is packed on to how many sledges at Trollesund?

11. Ruta Skadi wears a crown ringed with the teeth of which animal?

12. Who, in *The Subtle Knife*, is building a huge fortress with pieces of basalt rock half a hill in height?

13. On which continent does Mrs Coulter travel to see a type of slave called a Zombi?

14. What is the surname of the family of builders who have worked at Jordan College for five generations?

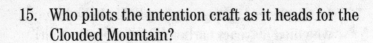

15. Who pilots the intention craft as it heads for the Clouded Mountain?

16. Onto whose sledge does Iorek Byrnison first place his armour after cleaning it?

17. What sound signals the end of the gyptians' Roping?

18. The person who shares a prison cell with Lyra in Svalbard was Regis Professor of Cosmology at what English university?

19. What injury is the badge of the bearer of the subtle knife?

20. Who does Iorek Byrnison's ship pick up as a passenger the first time they also pick up fuel?

21. In *Northern Lights*, by what transport is Lyra to leave Jordan College at dawn?

22. In *The Subtle Knife*, whose dæmon nearly gets through a gap in a window to another world cut by Will?

23. The Chevalier Tialys tells Lyra and Will that Mrs Coulter has been caught by the forces of which king?

24. In *Northern Lights*, what was the newer and shorter word used for the substance previously known as Rusakov Particles?

25. Are the Gallivespians the only human-like creatures in their own world or are there humans bigger than them?

26. Was Grumman sent up to the North by the Finnish Academy, the German Academy or the Lapland Academy?

27. Who does Lord Asriel say was a lover of Mrs Coulter?

28. In *Northern Lights*, the Northern Progress Exploration Company is really controlled by which board?

29. What aircraft does Lyra spot from the roof of Jordan College, heading for London?

30. The second bullet to really hurt Lee Scoresby hits: his right arm, his left leg, his chest or his right foot?

31. Whose dæmon is called Kulang: Sir Charles Latrom, Sebastian Makepeace, Ama or Lena Feldt?

32. Colonel Carborn made the first balloon flight over: the German Ocean, the Atlantic Ocean or the North Pole?

33. What object's actions cause Dust to leak out of a world?

34. Which member of Jordan College attempts to poison Lord Asriel?

35. When Lyra and Will finally find their dæmons surrounded by Spectres, are their dæmons in the form of rats, wildcats, tigers or eagles?

36. How many of the hands on the alethiometer can Lyra not control?

37. Was the intention craft built by the Magisterium, Iorek Byrnison or Lord Asriel's forces?

38. What colour is Iorek's armour the first time Lyra sees it?

39. Where was Iofur Raknison the king?

40. In *The Subtle Knife*, what does the Torre degli Angeli mean in English?

41. Does Will fear more than anything else that Lyra, his mother or his sister would be taken away?

42. Is it Dirk Vries, Raymond van Gerrit or Sam
     Broekman who suggests at the Roping that
     gyptians should not put themselves in danger
     to help a non-gyptian girl?

43. What item does Mrs Coulter use to open a door
     into the College of St Jerome?

44. Does the first bullet to really hurt Lee Scoresby
     strike his right thigh, his left ankle, his right
     wrist or his left shoulder?

45. Do all the different gyptian families meet in
     Hackney Marshes, the Fens or the Swamps of
     Southsea?

46. Who spies on the Consistorial Court of Discipline
     as they decide to kill Lyra?

47. Whose name is the last word Hester says before
     she and Lee Scoresby die?

48. Lyra receives a new coat in Trollesund, made of
     which animal's skin?

49. Just before the head of the gang of children and
     Will fight, whose dæmon arrives?

50. What does Lyra say Iofur has to do to win her as
     his dæmon?

1. Who steals the intention craft from Lord Asriel?

2. Moments after Madame Oxentiel arrives at the battle to aid Lyra and Will, which old friend of Lyra's comes with a force to help as well?

3. In *The Subtle Knife*, Lee Scoresby is attacked by a Skraeling after leaving: the Samirsky Hotel, the Imperial Muscovite Academy observatory or the fortress at Svalbard?

4. What is the name of the gyptian lady who had nursed Lyra at an early age?

5. Who orders all the harpies in the land of the dead to listen to the truth in every ghost's own story?

6. Which heavenly figure is a symbol on Lyra's alethiometer?

7. Who does the Master say is appointed executor of Lord Asriel's endowment to Lyra: Mrs Coulter, the Master, Mary Malone or John Faa?

8. In *Northern Lights*, who has a reward on their head of one thousand sovereigns?

9. Baruch draws a map for Will of where Lyra is hidden, which features a strange, winding glacier running between how many almost identical mountain peaks?

10. In which book does Mrs Coulter kill Lord Boreal?

11. Who uses a device at Jordan College that
     features an oil tank and a lens?

12. What word, beginning with the letter S, was
     used for the academics at Jordan College?

13. Which friend of Lyra's from *Northern Lights*
     enters the world containing Cittàgazze with
     Stanislaus Grumman?

14. Who digs their fingers into the eyes of the great
     angel, Metatron?

15. Does Jacob Huismans, Peter Hawker or
     Benjamin de Ruyter fall to his death from a high
     staircase?

16. In *The Amber Spyglass*, Roger tells Lyra that his
     death: was Lyra's fault, was not Lyra's fault or
     that both she and Roger made it happen?

17. In the book, *Lyra's Oxford*, what is the name of
     the college Lyra lived in during term time?

18. What animal is wounded before Lyra and Will's
     eyes, then healed to test the magic potion made
     by the witches?

19. Which alethiometer reader is pale and thin with a nightingale for his dæmon?

20. In *Northern Lights*, does the Witch-Consul tell the gyptians that a group of six, twelve, twenty-four or thirty-six children arrived recently?

21. In *The Amber Spyglass*, what must the townspeople sell the bears if Will manages to make the bears give way?

22. In *Northern Lights*, one of the rumours about Lyra was that she was spying and in the pay of: the Laplanders, the Tartars or the bears of Svalbard?

23. The Authority is the creator of all worlds: true or false?

24. What does Father Semyon say Will's name would be in Siberia?

25. Is the youngest member of the Consistorial Court of Discipline called Father Gomez, Father MacPhail or Father Makepwe?

26. Does Lyra have to hide for two hours beneath Ma, Tony or Billy Costa's bunk bed to avoid a police search?

27. In *Lyra's Oxford* was Makepeace a scholar at Jordan, Merton or Gabriel's College before he went mad?

28. Which great angel is determined to capture Lyra and Will's dæmons?

29. Which Gallivespian spy attacks the witch that had attacked Mrs Coulter, but dies from a fall?

30. In *Lyra's Oxford*, do Lyra and Pan spot Lord Asriel's dæmon, a witch's dæmon or Mrs Coulter's dæmon in a giant flock of birds?

31. Does Lyra first meet Iorek Byrnison in: Trollesund, Svalbard or at Bolvangar?

32. What alcoholic drink is Will forced to drink before leaving Father Semyon?

33. What is the first real object that Will cuts using the subtle knife?

34. What is the name of the child in *Northern Lights* who goes missing from the market in Oxford: Tony Makarios, Bella Gentleforth or Jessie Reynolds?

35. Sir Charles Latrom strikes a deal with Will and Lyra for them to return back with what object he really wants?

36. How many Spectres does Serafina Pekkala's dæmon say have surrounded the building on which Lyra and Will are trapped: over 30, over 60, over 100 or over 150?

37. Were females allowed into or always barred from the Retiring Room at Jordan College?

38. What is the name given to the giant birds that attacked the mulefa: grefari, poltari or tualapi?

39. At the great battle in *The Amber Spyglass*, what item does a horserider throw to entrap Iorek?

40. In *Lyra's Oxford*, were huge numbers of starlings, seagulls or geese roosting in the Botanic Gardens?

41. When Lee Scoresby and Grumman are trying to land, what type of tree does their basket catch and rest on?

42. What is the name of the angel who reluctantly pretends to be Will's dæmon at the start of *The Amber Spyglass*?

43. The men who guard the Experimental Station all have dæmons in the same animal form. What animal is it?

44. Is the lodestone resonator operated using a stylus, a series of switches or a bow?

45. Who tells Will that Lyra thinks Will is one of the bravest people she has ever seen?

46. Does Pantalaimon, Iorek or Thorold awaken Lyra to tell her that Lord Asriel has left his home in Svalbard?

47. Which commander of spies for Lord Asriel has a poisonous sting in his spurs?

48. What is the name of the first child to go missing in *Northern Lights*?

49. In *Lyra's Oxford*, how many years have passed since Will and Lyra parted?

50. Lady Salmakia's dragonfly has what power?

QUIZ 15

1. What is the name of the first town, beginning with the letter T, where the gyptians' ship lands after leaving England?

2. Whose mother's ring does Stanislaus Grumman have: Lyra's, Will's, Giacomo's or Lee Scoresby's?

3.   What is the name of the weapon used by Iorek's bears, which features an iron tank and a bowl a yard in diameter?

4.   In *Lyra's Oxford*, Lyra invents a reason for going to visit Sebastian Makepeace. Is it: to get help with her homework, to get some treacle toffee or to collect a flute?

5.   What, beginning with the letter R, was the name of Tony Makarios's missing dæmon?

6.   At the meeting of the gyptians, where Lyra first sees John Faa, how many men are on the platform: three, eight or fourteen?

7.   Who performs mental magic to make themselves almost invisible before spying on a meeting including Mrs Coulter, Fra Pavel and others?

8.   What sort of wood is the handle of the subtle knife made from?

9.   In *The Subtle Knife*, Serafina Pekkala leads the witches in a chant and spell to heal the injuries of which person?

10. When Dr Malone asks Atal how long the mulefa had lived, does she answer: 4000 years, 11,000 years or 33,000 years?

11. Who is the first person Will meets in Cittàgazze?

12. Grimmsdur was the name of what kind of creature killed by a harpoon on display at the Royal Arctic Institute?

13. Whose dæmon gets almost all of Lyra's hair out of the bomb?

14. At the start of his lecture to the Jordan College scholars, does Lord Asriel say his expedition to the North began three, six, nine or twelve months ago?

15. What object do the shadow particles tell Dr Malone to find before she must deceive a guardian?

16. Who teaches Mary Malone to see her own dæmon?

17. At the very start of *Northern Lights*, in which part of Jordan College is Lyra: the Hall, the Retiring Room or the kitchens?

18. Who spends many hours studying the subtle knife on a river voyage: Iorek, Will or Mrs Coulter?

19. What colour were the uniforms of the military men fighting Lee Scoresby in *The Subtle Knife*?

20. Who tells Mrs Coulter that in past years he became a spy?

21. In *The Subtle Knife*, which room in his house does Will first search for the leather writing case?

22. Was it traditional for the Chaplain, the Master or the Butler to cook poppy in butter after a feast?

23. Who steals matches from the kitchen at Bolvangar: Lyra, Roger, Iorek or Billy Costa?

24. By what first name does Mrs Coulter call Sir Charles Latrom in *The Subtle Knife*?

25. Which one of the following items does Will not take from the campsite containing the dead body of Lord Boreal: Kendal Mint Cake, a whistle, an electric torch, a pair of binoculars?

26. Who does Father MacPhail order to follow the tempter to find Lyra?

27. What is the name of the member of the Costa family who has gone missing, presumed taken by the Gobblers?

28. Who keeps watch whilst Will breaks into Sir Charles Latrom's house?

29. On the voyage to Trollesund, Lyra gets a little
    fearful about Pantalaimon wanting to stay as
    what sort of creature forever?

30. Alethiometers are said to have originated in
    which European city: Oslo, Prague, Berlin or
    Athens?

31. Are the human crew who sailed Iorek's boat
    friendly, nasty or indifferent to Will?

32. When captured in Svalbard, Lyra asks the
    alethiometer how far away Iorek is. How many
    days does the alethiometer reply?

33. What object does Dr Malone use to smash part
    of the Cave computer?

34. What job did Lyra's friend, Roger, perform at
    Jordan College?

35. Which angel does Lord Asriel wrestle, with both
    of them falling into the abyss?

36. Who is queen of the witch clan in the Lake
    Enara region?

37. When did the Spectres arrive in large numbers
    in Cittàgazze and other parts of that world:
    100, 300, 500 or 700 years ago?

38. Who is wearing khaki hunting clothes when she kills a witch and a Lord from Lyra's world?

39. The alethiometers are said to have been made in which century: 15th, 17th, 19th or 20th?

40. Is Sophonax the name of John Faa's, Lord Asriel's or Farder Coram's dæmon?

41. What word, beginning with the letter A, is another name for the Northern Lights?

42. Lyra wears a little white leather shoulder bag almost all the time she lives with Mrs Coulter. What does she always put in it?

43. Does Iorek wear his armour when he takes Lyra into the village north of Trollesund to rescue the boy?

44. What is the name of the plant used to help treat wounds on bears: liverwort, bloodmoss or heal-leaf?

45. How many gold dollars does Lord Asriel give Lyra when he visits her in Oxford?

46. How many witches does Serafina Pekkala originally select to fly with her into the new world: 13, 20, 32 or 50?

47. What happens to people's dæmons as they become adults?

48. The Authority's Regent is called: Balthamos, Metatron or Adonai?

49. After being used, how long does it take for the poisoned spurs of Lord Roke to rebuild their maximum strength?

50. Stew and mashed potatoes is the first meal Lyra eats: on board the Costas' boat, with Mrs Coulter or at the Experimental Station?

QUIZ 16

1. Which alethiometer symbol does Lyra think represents hard work: the anchor, the beehive or the helmet?

2. At their first meeting Mrs Coulter excites Lyra with tales of negotiating with which land's witches: Svalbard, Lapland or Trollesund?

3. In *The Subtle Knife*, do Spectres attack dæmons, children or adults?

4. In which compass direction was the ship going, taking the captured children out of Brytain?

5.   Does the witch tortured on board the ship containing Mrs Coulter have both of her arms or both of her legs broken?

6.   What item of identification of Oliver Payne's does Dr Malone use to fool the policeman?

7.   Will's father had last been heard from when he accompanied an archaeological expedition. Was it called the Nuniatak, Asaqatuk or Nebula dig?

8.   Which Lord does John Faa tell the Roping is a good friend of the gyptians?

9.   Who is tied to a chair with their clothing torn, in Lord Asriel's tower?

10. After passing Cittàgazze, what do Lee Scoresby and Grumman spot in the air?

11. What is the name of the old gyptian man who walks on sticks and is an advisor of John Faa?

12. What famous book, according to Lord Asriel, gave the particles their name of Dust?

13. Which two people, whose meeting in Jordan College was secretly watched by Lyra, were on the Cabinet Council, a body which advised the Prime Minister?

14. Xaphania is an ally of Lord Asriel; what sort of creature is Xaphania?

15. How many squadron of gyropters does Lord Asriel order to the air after meeting with Baruch?

16. What is the name of the big publishers in *Lyra's Oxford*: Fell Press, Ashmolean Books or the Pitt-Rivers Press?

17. What is the name of the village girl who brings Mrs Coulter and Lyra food when they are in hiding in the Himalayas?

18. Does Will lose his little finger, his middle finger or his thumb?

19. Was Simon Hartmann, Dirk Vries or Benjamin de Ruyter put in charge of spying for the gyptians by John Faa?

20. Who must fly Stanislaus Grumman into the world Lord Asriel has opened?

21. How many alethiometers does the Master say were made?

22. Whose father does Stanislaus Grumman turn out to be?

23. In *Lyra's Oxford*, what sort of bird roosted on St Michael's Tower?

24. Which human, arriving at the Clouded Mountain, sees the Authority being carried on a litter by angels?

25. In *Northern Lights*, who is Lyra to leave Jordan College and live with?

26. In *The Subtle Knife*, are the reports of the numbers in Lord Asriel's army in the hundreds, thousands or millions?

27. Who has found a way of preserving bloodmoss in an ointment to heal wounds?

28. When Lyra first meets Iorek Byrnison, he is gnawing the leg meat of what animal?

29. The gyptian boy, Charlie, said he saw Gobblers in: Banbury, Reading, Swindon or Woking?

30. What is the first drink Will takes and pays for in the new world he enters?

31. In *Lyra's Oxford*, which of the following colleges was furthest north: Durham, Gabriel, St Sophia's or Foxe?

32. In *Northern Lights*, which is the most powerful force in Lyra's country: the Church, businessmen or the King and Queen?

33. In *The Subtle Knife*, can you name either of the odd things Mrs Cooper spots about Will's mother's face?

34. Is Cousins the name of the manservant of: the Master, Lord Asriel, John Faa or The Intercessor?

35. According to the witches' prophecy, what will Lyra become like: Eve, the devil or the Authority?

36. Who does Lyra first surprise by her knowledge of Dust?

37. When Lyra asks the alethiometer how to get to the land of the dead, what object does the alethiometer tell her to follow?

38. Who begged the court that tried Lord Asriel to let her keep the baby Lyra and bring her up: Mrs Coulter, Ma Costa or Serafina Pekkala?

39. How many of Lord Asriel's spies are in the zeppelin carrying the President of the Consistorial Court?

40. In what colour is the Master usually dressed?

41. In *Lyra's Oxford*, who does the witch's dæmon say has visited Sebastian Makepeace in the past: Lord Asriel, Dr Lanselius or Serafina Pekkala?

42. In the new world Mary Malone enters, what appears to be on the end of the legs of the animals with short trunks and horned heads?

43. When the gang of 40 or more children come to attack Lyra and Will, their leader is a boy in a striped t-shirt carrying what weapon?

44. At the start of the book, *Lyra's Oxford*, is Pantalaimon in the form of a pine marten, a squirrel, a seagull or a cat?

45. Who stole the subtle knife from Giacomo Paradisi?

46. In *Lyra's Oxford* did Yelena Pazhets's son fight for or against Lord Asriel in the late war?

47. How many days north-east of Trollesund does Kaisa tell Farder Coram the Experimental Station is?

48. By what nickname, which includes a bird's name, is Cittàgazze known?

49. How old was Will when he learned that his mother was different and needed looking after?

50. What is the name of the wine that is poured especially for Lord Asriel at the start of *Northern Lights*?

QUIZ 17

1. Who does Lee Scoresby call for help just before he dies?

2. What is the name of the female scholar Lyra seeks out in *The Subtle Knife*?

3. What soft drink does Will find for Lyra the first time they meet?

4. Who does the Consistorial Court of Discipline send on a mission to kill Lyra?

5. In *The Subtle Knife*, which one of Lyra's friends makes his way to the Samirsky Hotel to find out more about where Stanislaus Grumman is?

6. With what does Lord Asriel bribe the bears of Svalbard to build the exact house he wants in Svalbard?

7. Is Kholodnoye in Lapland, Siberia, Nippon or Norroway?

8. Does Lord Asriel drink the bottle of Tokay left for him by the Master of Jordan College?

9. Does Xaphania tell Lyra that it will take a year, ten years or a lifetime to regain her abilities to read the alethiometer?

10. What sort of animal takes Lyra prisoner after she falls out of Lee Scoresby's balloon?

11. The gate to the land of the dead lies: at the top of a mountain, on an island, deep underground or high in the air?

12. In *Northern Lights*, what is the name of the creature with leathery wings and hooked claws which attacks Lee Scoresby's balloon?

13. Did Mrs Coulter convince the King, the Prime Minister or the Church to pay for the Experimental Station at Bolvangar?

14. Who was reading the alethiometer on board the ship containing Mrs Coulter: Stanislaus Grumman, Fra Pavel, Cardinal Hurz or Sam Cansino?

15. Who accompanied Simon Parslow and Hugh Lovat when they learned of one of the gyptian children having been taken by the Gobblers?

16. On their first night journeying from Trollesund, what animal's meat do Lyra and the others eat, roasted?

17. Will finds a way into another world close to a row of unusually-shaped: chestnut, oak, hornbeam or sycamore trees?

18. Is Adèle Starminster a dancer, a journalist or a scholar?

19. What does Will wrap around his hand during his fight with Tullio?

20. When the Costa family meets Lyra in London, is Ma Costa's dæmon in the form of a grey dog or a red fox?

21. The gyptian spies in London catch three Gobblers in: White Hall, Folkeshall or Clerkenwell?

22. Who swaps gold coins for Yak leather boots and a sheepskin waistcoat in *The Amber Spyglass*?

23. Whose manservant is Thorold?

24. Do Lyra and Will plan to visit the Botanic Gardens each year on Midsummer's Day, the Autumn Equinox, Christmas Day or the first day of Spring?

25. According to Mary Malone, Alfredo Montale was: the man she had loved, her priest or her boss at the Dark Matter Research Unit?

26. Is Dr Dee who lives on the banks of the River Isis a great surgeon, explorer or magician?

27. In *Lyra's Oxford* where does Lyra take the injured swan after the fight with the witch?

28. The Costa family were members of which gyptian family: Stefanski, Stanza or Van Gerrit?

29. Is the oldest member of the Consistorial Court of Discipline called Father MacPhail, Father Makepwe or Dr Cooper?

30. In which of the books do we first meet Lee Scoresby?

31. Who does Tony Costa tell Lyra is the king of the gyptians?

32. In *The Subtle Knife*, into whose car does Lyra head in order to escape the police chasing her?

33. Although he hates killing, how many times had Lee Scoresby killed before he starts searching for Stanislaus Grumman?

34. When the children are escaping from the Experimental Station at Bolvangar, which group starts to fire arrows on the Tartars?

35. Who manages to trick Iofur in combat by pretending their arm is damaged?

36. Who saves Lyra when she falls as she is leading the ghosts out of the land of the dead?

37. The first time Lyra and Will visit Sir Charles Latrom's house, into which room are they shown: the drawing room, the study or the attic?

38. Who uses a rifle to become the first human to shoot and kill a tualapi?

39. Which was the last ghost Will talked to before following Lyra and their dæmons into another world?

40. What sort of animal does Iorek kill and share with Will during their walk up the valley in *The Amber Spyglass*?

41. In *The Amber Spyglass*, which old friend guides Lyra to her dæmon, taking over from Iorek?

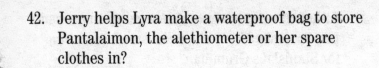

42. Jerry helps Lyra make a waterproof bag to store Pantalaimon, the alethiometer or her spare clothes in?

43. What actually are the wheels that the Mulefa use to travel around?

44. How many balloons does Lee Scoresby have with him in *Northern Lights*?

45. In what city does Lyra live after leaving Oxford?

46. Whose dead body does Lyra hold in her arms as she sees her parents together for the first time?

47. Anfang is the dæmon of which servant: Thorold, the Porter or Mrs Lonsdale?

48. Who makes a meal of omelette and baked beans in Cittàgazze?

49. Who is Sir Charles Latrom's guest the night Will breaks into his house?

50. In *The Subtle Knife*, what do Mrs Coulter's soldiers lack?

QUIZ 18

1. In *Northern Lights*, what is the name of the main port of Lapland?

2. In what European country had Mary Malone been giving an academic paper when she fell in love with an Italian man?

3. Who does Grumman tell Will he must go to with the subtle knife?

4. At the end of *The Subtle Knife* after Will has climbed to a plateau, someone grabs him: by his left leg, neck or right arm?

5. When Will cuts his first opening into another world, can you name either of the two people who are with him?

6. Who has retired to a chamber of crystal and lets someone else run his kingdom?

7. Does Lydia Alexandrovna live in Kholodnoye, Oxford or Svalbard?

8. The key that locks Mrs Coulter's handcuffs on the journey through the Alps is: short and stubby with black tape around it, long and thin and painted yellow or large and fashioned from pure silver?

9. Is the lodestone resonator a device used to send messages between Lyra and Will, between Lord Asriel's spies or between gyptian boats?

10. In *The Amber Spyglass*, who does Serafina Pekkala go to see after finding Lee Scoresby dead?

11. In *The Subtle Knife*, soldiers from a number of different worlds are coming together to join whose army?

12. Who was the first creature that Iofur Raknison had ever killed?

13. Who gives Lyra a small twig of cloud-pine from the spray used by Serafina Pekkala?

14. Is the police inspector who questions Lyra in Dr Malone's university building called: Griffiths, Johnson or Walters?

15. What is the name of the witch who sends Farder Coram help after he has been shot with a poison arrow by the Skraelings?

16. What figures were carved on the mysterious tower in the middle of Cittàgazze?

17. What was the name of Mrs Coulter's husband?

18. Who is saved, by a cat, from capture by Mrs Coulter and Sir Charles Latrom?

19. Can you name either the red-haired brother or sister that Lyra and Will first encounter near the harbour of Cittàgazze?

20. Who, after some thought, does Serafina Pekkala think might be Æsahættr?

21. Is the Master of Jordan College over 50, over 60, over 70 or over 80?

22. In *Northern Lights*, which nobleman does Lord Boreal say has been imprisoned in a fortress at Svalbard?

23. What is the name of the ocean that the gyptians' ship first sails into?

24. Who is Lyra supposed to keep the alethiometer away from?

25. People at the College of St Jerome make a special bomb designed to destroy: The Authority, Will, Mrs Coulter or Lyra?

26. Mrs Coulter is taken in handcuffs to the power generating station in what sort of transport?

27. Which other spy does the Chevalier Tialys meet at their agreed seventh meeting place?

28. The soles of Lyra's new boots from Trollesund are made from the skin of: a walrus, a bearded seal or a reindeer?

29. Who first pilots the intention craft and destroys a raiding party?

30. Was the Anbaric Park Lyra knew of, on the road to Cowley, Yarnton or Banbury?

31. What device does Lyra unleash on Mrs Coulter just after Mrs Coulter asks her for the alethiometer?

32. What was Metatron's previous name, beginning with the letter E?

33. Which friend of Lyra's is superb at fashioning metals?

34. Apart from Lyra, how many other females were on board the gyptians' ship that set sail for the North?

35. What vintage is the special Tokay wine that Lord Asriel is particularly fond of: 1762, 1898, 1913 or 1954?

36. What is the name of Will's pet: Macie, Moxie or Mannie?

37. Which character in *The Subtle Knife* lives in Limefield House?

38. Do the gyptians, witches or armoured bears kill 22 guards and 9 staff at Bolvangar?

39. Pantalaimon's favourite form to sleep as is: a mouse, a cat, an ermine or a hamster?

40. How many shots did Lord Asriel fire at Edward Coulter?

41. Which of the witches was 416 years old: Ruta Skadi, Juta Kamainen or Serafina Pekkala?

42. Which local girl shows Iorek and Will the cave containing Lyra?

43. What does Farder Coram first offer Iorek Byrnison to come on the expedition: gold, the throne of Svalbard or his own ship?

44. Who does Lyra have to leave behind at the snow bridge to pursue Lord Asriel?

45. Who first shows a picture of Dust flowing around a person in the North: Mrs Coulter, Lord Asriel or John Faa?

46. When Lee and Grumman return to the port in *The Subtle Knife*, they find the place overrun with soldiers from: Norroway, Lapland, Svalbard or Muscovy?

47. Who tells Lyra that she is, after all, coming on the gyptians' expedition to the North?

48. The first meaning of the ant symbol on the alethiometer is: trapped, busy, powerless or banding together?

49. What vehicle does Lord Asriel use to carry Roger and his instruments away from his home in Svalbard?

50. Who did Giacomo Paradisi try to lure into Cittàgazze with an opening between the worlds?

QUIZ 19

1. When Lee Scoresby reloads during the battle with the Muscovy soldiers, which creature's tears nearly break his heart?

2. Who does Father MacPhail first plan to cut from their dæmon to provide energy for the bomb to kill Lyra?

3. Who does Lyra see empty a powder into a bottle of wine in the Retiring Room?

4. The first time Serafina and the other witches see Spectres attacking a group of people, how many riders flee the Spectres, leaving the others to be attacked?

5. Who does John Faa put in charge of finding and commanding a ship to sail to the North: Nicholas Rokeby, Adam Stefanski or Farder Coram?

6. Which of the Jordan College scholars is nearly blind: the Librarian, the Chaplain or the Sub-Rector?

7. How long do Will and Lyra voyage on the gyptians' boat together before they have to part?

8. How many angels meet Will moments after his father dies?

9. Who does Mrs Coulter insist on having a meeting with at the College of St Jerome?

10. Who wades into the river to save five of the seedpods used by the mulefa?

11. Why was Iorek exiled from Svalbard?

12. Which desperately ill angel insists on speaking to Lord Asriel in *The Amber Spyglass*?

13. When Dr Malone asks the shadow-particles what they are, using the computer, what is their one word answer, beginning with the letter A?

14. Grumman tells Lee Scoresby how the enemy is going to find them. Is it by burning the forest, using spy-flies or using renegade witches?

15. When confronted by Lyra, Sir Charles Latrom denies he has taken her alethiometer: true or false?

16. What colour is the leather writing case Will searches for?

17. Who works at a sledge depot in Trollesund before joining Lyra and the others in their quest?

18. What item do the witches on Lord Asriel's side use to attack the angels?

19. Who buys a clipboard, pad of paper and a pen so as not to arouse suspicion, in *The Subtle Knife*?

20. In what sort of black material is the alethiometer wrapped?

21. The first time Will puts the subtle knife to the throat of a witch, is the witch Lena Feldt, Juta Kamainen or Serafina Pekkala?

22. What is the occupation of the man who welcomes Will into his house in the Siberian village?

23. With which group of Lyra's allies had Serafina Pekkala come into the world of the mulefa?

24. Lee Scoresby fills his balloon up using gas from Mrs Coulter's airship: true or false?

25. What is the name of Ama's dæmon?

26. What does the man breaking in to Will's house trip over, and fall down the stairs as a result?

27. How many thousands of years ago was Metatron appointed as Regent to the Authority?

28. How many shillings does the coffee and ham sandwich she buys in a London street cost Lyra?

29. How many people can Lee Scoresby and his balloon carry: three, six or ten?

30. What other word is used to describe the Clouded Mountain: the Chariot, the Peak of Fear or the Homecoming?

31. What is the name of the collection of courts and councils set up by the church: the Tribunalia, the Supreme Inquisitor or the Magisterium?

32. When Lyra is thinking about the gyptians' spy, she chooses three symbols on the alethiometer. Can you name one of them?

33. Who says to Lyra that if people like Mrs Coulter think that Dust is bad, maybe it is good?

34. What animal symbol on the alethiometer means Asia?

35. Which of the Jordan College scholars, on seeing one of Lord Asriel's slides, thinks that it looks like a city in the air?

36. At the very start of *Northern Lights*, is Pantalaimon in the form of a wildcat, a dove, a moth or a mouse?

37. What item do the two Gallivespian spies leave in Will and Lyra's care as a sign of trust?

38. Is Pagdzin *tulku* first encountered in *Lyra's Oxford*, *The Amber Spyglass* or *The Subtle Knife*?

39. Does Mrs Coulter lure Tony into a trap with the promise of chocolatl, five gold sovereigns or a tray of pastries?

40. What simple meal on toast does Will make for himself in his last night at his home?

41. Who tells Iorek Byrnison where his armour is hidden?

42. What item of Mrs Coulter's jewellery does Brother Louis take from her body while she is sleeping?

43. Which of the children had found a hiding place in the Experimental Station above the ceiling panels?

44. Are most dæmons the same sex as, or the opposite sex to, their human?

45. Do the Gallivespians have dæmons that others can see?

46. How many guns does the town which attacks Iorek's boat have?

47. Lord Asriel is surprised to hear that Lyra and Will's lost dæmons have been sighted. Are the dæmons first in the form of: nightingales, cats, doves or mice?

48. What sort of creatures do Lyra and Will help Mary Malone gather for the mulefa to eat: molluscs, fireflies, gazelle or fish?

49. Do the balloons chasing Lee Scoresby in
     The Subtle Knife come from the south, east
     or west?

50. In *Northern Lights*, what vehicle of Mrs
     Coulter's do the bears under Iorek's
     command destroy?

HARD QUESTIONS

1. When Lyra finally returns to her own Oxford, whose collection of valuable silver has been looted?

2. What was the name of the bear that Iorek Byrnison killed, resulting in his exile from Svalbard?

3. On what object does the man in Will's house crack his head, resulting in his death?

4. In *Northern Lights*, the author made a mistake and gave the dæmon of one adult character two different forms. Can you name the character?

5. Can you name both forms that the above character's dæmon takes?

6. When Mary and Will return to their Oxford, what is the thing that Mary says she most wants?

7. In *Lyra's Oxford*, who found their own son killed with one of their own arrows?

8. What is the name of the female Gallivespian who takes over the command after Lord Roke dies?

9. What are the first words the shadow particles display on the Cave computer?

10. Where in Trollesund was Iorek's armour hidden?

11. In *Lyra's Oxford*, what is the name of the witch's dæmon that Lyra and Pan rescued?

12. What two metals made the alloy of the guillotine blade used to separate children from their dæmons at the Experimental Station?

13. Who uses an alethiometer to tell Mrs Coulter that her daughter is still alive after the bomb?

14. What new name does Lyra give the harpy, No-Name?

15. Teleutaia makhaira is another name for what object?

16. In *Lyra's Oxford*, what is the name of the scholar Lyra sat down to dinner with?

17. What is the name of the first man that Will and Lyra meet who is dead, before they follow the ghosts?

18. In *The Amber Spyglass*, how old is Mrs Coulter?

19. Who commands Lord Asriel's air force that seeks out Lyra?

20. What is the currency in the new world Will enters?

21. Which angel approaches Will and Lyra just after Lyra loses her power to read the alethiometer?

22. What is the name of the first village, beginning with the letter K, that Will and Balthamos come across?

23. What is the name of the witch in *The Subtle Knife* who has a snow bunting for a dæmon?

24. What flavour soup is Will served at the Siberian priest's house?

25. What is the name of the lady Lyra meets at the end of *The Amber Spyglass*, who is head of one of the women's colleges?

26. What title at Jordan College did Ignatius Cole and Simon Le Clerc both have in the past?

27. What two words do Angelica and Paolo use to describe witches?

28. How many child mulefa are there in the village where Mary Malone stays?

29. What bird-like name does the Butler at Jordan College have?

30. Who does John Faa make second in command of the entire gyptian expedition to the North?

31. How many gyptian men does John Faa announce were to head to the North?

32. In *Lyra's Oxford*, what is the first name of the girl who asks Lyra to a flute recital?

33. What sort of wood has a tiring effect on dæmons, making them fall asleep?

34. Can you name either of the nuns who act as stenographers in the Consistorial Court of Discipline, writing down everything that is said?

35. What is the name of the witches' goddess of the dead?

36. What is the name, beginning with the letter S, of the oldest of the mulefa?

37. What is the name of the bank Lee Scoresby sends gold back to after every job he does?

38. In *Lyra's Oxford*, what is the name of the young male scholar who knew about Sebastian Makepeace?

39. To prove Lyra is a dæmon, Iofur asks her questions. Can you recall what the first question is?

40. What is the name of the medical woman who is the first at Bolvangar to see Lyra's alethiometer?

41. What is the name of the Oxford museum in which Lyra sees some skulls and dates them as much older than the Bronze Age?

42. How many heavy coins does a man at the Experimental Station give to Lyra's kidnappers?

43. What is the name of the pass through which Will and Iorek have to travel to reach Lyra?

44. What does Will spot coming out from the cuff of Sir Charles Latrom's linen jacket?

45. Who puts his hands on Lyra's shoulder at the side of the canal in *Lyra's Oxford*?

46. What year were all of John Parry's letters to his wife dated?

47. What false name does Will give to the adults after Lyra has been involved in a road accident?

48. What creature tells a cliff-ghast that the bear-King was heading south, just before the cliff-ghast eats it?

49. What is the name of the man who reads the alethiometer for Lord Asriel?

50. What species of bird does Balthamos turn into the first time Will asks him to pretend to be his dæmon?

EASY
ANSWERS

1. Lyra
2. Philip Pullman
3. A witch
4. A bear
5. *The Subtle Knife*
6. Dæmons
7. Will and Lyra
8. Her uncle
9. Oxford
10. *Northern Lights*

11. A hot-air balloon
12. No
13. His left hand
14. Canal boats
15. Roger
16. Will
17. Africa
18. Will's
19. Pantalaimon
20. Shorter

21. Dust
22. Mrs Coulter
23. A fire person
24. *The Amber Spyglass*
25. Will

26. False
27. Her father
28. Black
29. *The Subtle Knife*
30. London

31. False
32. Lord Asriel
33. A gyptian
34. Will
35. Pan
36. Iorek
37. No
38. Mary Malone
39. Roger
40. Lyra

41. Oxford
42. Spectres
43. Jordan College
44. Cittàgazze
45. Alethiometer
46. A widow
47. *Northern Lights*
48. A dog
49. Dust
50. Lord Asriel

MEDIUM
ANSWERS

1. Cittàgazze
2. Her last breakfast
3. False
4. Dr Mary Malone
5. Will's father
6. One hundred pounds
7. Sugar
8. Downwards
9. Lyra
10. His fingertips (fingers)

11. The Sheldon Building
12. The Costas
13. A cliff-ghast
14. Roger and Lyra
15. A bag of wheel-tree seeds, some wheel-tree oil
16. Poppy
17. A horserider from *The Subtle Knife*
18. Stanislaus Grumman
19. A robin
20. Two

21. Mrs Coulter
22. Ama
23. God-destroyer
24. A hare

25. Angels
26. True
27. Fra Pavel
28. Female
29. Four
30. Lord Roke

31. A harpy
32. The Royal Marines
33. 17 Swiss Guards
34. A church
35. Lyra
36. Lord Asriel
37. Mrs Coulter
38. Lyra
39. Mrs Coulter
40. Cloud-pine

41. False
42. Ma Costa
43. A nun
44. Panserbørne
45. Scottish
46. The subtle knife
47. Swiss Guard
48. Serafina Pekkala
49. Mary Malone
50. They must be closed

QUIZ 2

1. Dark
2. Twenty pounds
3. White
4. Roger
5. The witches
6. Mrs Coulter
7. Electric
8. Lee Scoresby and Iorek Byrnison
9. Alan Perkins
10. The worst in everyone

11. Never open without closing, never let anyone else use it
12. Three times
13. A rag doll
14. Farder Coram, Iorek Byrnison
15. Lizards
16. Will
17. A spy for Lord Asriel
18. John Parry/Grumman
19. Greater distances
20. Their heart

21. Lee Scoresby
22. The Botanic Gardens
23. The Cave

24. John Parry
25. Gyptian
26. History
27. Witches
28. Lord Asriel
29. John Faa
30. Lyra

31. A piece of fish
32. Four
33. South-west
34. Will's father
35. His cloak
36. True
37. London
38. Yes
39. Brandy
40. Serafina Pekkala

41. The Spectres
42. Mrs Coulter
43. Tullio
44. True
45. Ruta Skadi
46. The Royal Arctic Institute
47. Destroy her
48. By drinking poison
49. A human head
50. Eels

QUIZ 3

1. Four
2. Tullio
3. Kirjava
4. Two
5. Angels
6. A uniformed guard
7. Svalbard
8. Three
9. Four times a year
10. A dæmon

11. Sir Charles Latrom
12. Lightning
13. A dancer
14. Geneva
15. Lyra, Mary Malone
16. A woman
17. Seal blubber
18. Mrs Coulter's
19. A boy from Limehouse
20. Lord Asriel

21. Ivan
22. A policewoman
23. Lord Roke
24. Fra Pavel
25. A train

26. The mulefa
27. Lee Scoresby
28. Spectres
29. A cheetah
30. False

31. Sky-iron
32. Honey
33. Female
34. A film at a cinema
35. Gold
36. Stanislaus Grumman
37. A harmless camomile drink
38. Serafina Pekkala
39. Gabriel College,
    St Martin's College
40. The land of the dead

41. Mary Malone
42. Lee Scoresby
43. She is seasick
44. Einarsson's Bar
45. Jacob Huismans
46. A Tartar
47. Lord Asriel
48. The Oblation Board
49. A staircase
50. Mulefa

QUIZ 4

1. Farder Coram
2. The Porter
3. Sledges
4. The Master
5. Siberia
6. The Royal Arctic Institute
7. Oliver Payne
8. Copper
9. Clouded Mountain
10. By sledge

11. Lady Salmakia
12. The Watercourse Bill
13. Lyra
14. Because they are not dead
15. The Retiring Room
16. Never venture into the water
17. The Costa family's
18. The Librarian
19. Six
20. Lee Scoresby

21. He is pure gyptian blood
22. Spring and Autumn
23. Lyra
24. Lee Scoresby
25. Baruch

26. Old Headington
27. Intercision
28. Baruch
29. Giacomo Paradisi
30. Manchester

31. Iorek Byrnison
32. Lord Asriel
33. Blue
34. Angelica
35. The Chevalier Tialys
36. Lyra
37. The Master's
38. Nearly 1000 years old
39. The North
40. Father MacPhail

41. The Steward
42. *Lyra's Oxford*
43. A pie
44. Serafina Pekkala, Lyra and Lee Scoresby
45. Dr Broken Arrow
46. Tartars
47. Beds of herbs, a fountain
48. Mrs Coulter
49. King Ogunwe
50. Stanislaus Grumman

QUIZ 5

1. Balthamos
2. *Northern Lights*
3. Tony Makarios
4. Sheep
5. The Master
6. Lord Asriel
7. Parry
8. The third airship
9. Stones
10. A café

11. Roger
12. 60
13. Will
14. Mary Malone
15. Tartan
16. Shuter
17. An old rowing boat
18. Ten minutes
19. Stanislaus Grumman
20. An elephant

21. By boat
22. Spectre-orphans
23. Cremated
24. Bloodmoss
25. Tokay
26. Balthamos

27. Father MacPhail
28. A witch
29. Silvertongue
30. Jotham Santelia

31. Martha
32. The gyptians
33. A seagull
34. Dust
35. Ruta Skadi
36. Trollesund
37. Gobblers
38. Red and white
39. Lord Asriel
40. True

41. Iorek Byrnison
42. Green
43. Nova Zembla
44. Lyra
45. A Spectre
46. Bears
47. A piano teacher
48. Much smaller than regular humans
49. Will, the Chevalier Tialys and Lady Salmakia
50. Green

QUIZ 6

1. Mrs Coulter
2. A revolver
3. Bear
4. Chameleon
5. They started to melt
6. A stream
7. Tullio
8. Nine years old
9. His father
10. Will

11. Roger
12. Lyra
13. South
14. Serafina Pekkala
15. Lee Scoresby
16. Lyra
17. On a gyptian narrow-boat
18. Pantalaimon
19. The head (the skull)
20. Juta Kamainen

21. To steal
22. Six legs
23. Skraeling
24. Mary Malone
25. A range of hills

26. A train
27. Ama
28. Twelve members
29. Count
30. Jordan

31. Iorek Byrnison
32. A truck
33. Dragonflies
34. The Palmerian Professor
35. The Sub-Enquirer
36. A floppy disk
37. Hired it by paying in gold
38. Farder Coram, John Faa
39. Will Parry
40. Scalp

41. Sunderland Avenue
42. Granite
43. His leg
44. Nippon
45. Flautist
46. Tony Makarios
47. *Northern Lights*
48. Æsahættr
49. Ruta Skadi
50. A mouse

QUIZ 7

1. Farder Coram
2. Will
3. A cat
4. The Master
5. An arrow
6. The Breathless Ones
7. At a meeting of gyptians
8. Pagdzin *tulku*
9. Lord Asriel
10. A panama hat

11. Yes, one
12. The serpent
13. Balthamos
14. Balthamos, Baruch
15. John Faa
16. By the Claybeds
17. Milk
18. Her Swiss Army knife
19. Bolvangar
20. The Africans

21. His balloon
22. Iofur Raknison
23. Her hands
24. Leaves
25. White Hall

26. Death
27. Adam Stefanski
28. The governor
29. Fourteen
30. A holy woman

31. Will
32. Simon Hartmann
33. A senior politician
34. A porcupine
35. Lyra
36. Stew
37. An old shopping bag
38. Iofur Raknison
39. Dry matches
40. A cliff-ghast

41. Lena Feldt
42. Never use it for a base purpose, keep it secret
43. Iorek Byrnison
44. Mrs Cooper
45. Mrs Coulter
46. The underground vaults
47. Sewing
48. Xaphania
49. Iofur Raknison
50. Geneva

QUIZ 8

1. A cat
2. Spectres
3. Mary Malone
4. His armour
5. Stanislaus Grumman's dæmon
6. The final airship
7. One
8. Ruta Skadi
9. Hope
10. Atal

11. Dark green
12. A bird
13. Zalif
14. Tony Costa
15. In an air accident
16. Continue on foot
17. Mrs Coulter's dæmon
18. Dr Cooper, Fra Pavel, Father MacPhail
19. Staircase Twelve
20. Iorek Byrnison

21. Joyce
22. Dr Cooper
23. A swan
24. The subtle knife

25. Over 300 years old
26. His mother's ring
27. Sir Charles Latrom
28. Father Gomez
29. Billy Costa
30. One

31. A rifle
32. Lord Roke
33. Chthonic Railway
34. The Tower of the Angels
35. Eight inches
36. A ghost dog
37. Pantalaimon
38. I Ching
39. The Witch-Consul
40. A Spectre

41. Lyra
42. The fire bell
43. Metatron
44. Lord Asriel
45. Deodorant
46. The Royal Arctic Institute
47. A cat
48. A serpent
49. Lyra
50. A witch

QUIZ 9

1. John Faa
2. Svalbard
3. A skull
4. 38 men
5. A healer
6. Almost 40 years
7. The Madonna
8. Serafina Pekkala
9. Fifteen
10. Baruch

11. The zeppelin from Oxford
12. Lyra
13. The cinema
14. Lee Scoresby's
15. Mary Malone
16. A bat
17. Computer
18. The subtle knife
19. Iorek Byrnison
20. A journalist

21. Hydrogen
22. A frog
23. Stanislaus Grumman
24. Lord Boreal
25. Yaxley Quad

26. Charles
27. Mrs Coulter
28. His mother
29. Airships
30. Abingdon

31. A battle
32. Mrs Lonsdale
33. Geneva
34. Nicholas Rokeby
35. Mary Malone
36. The harpy
37. Iofur's lower jaw
38. Bolvangar
39. Dust
40. Gyropters

41. After
42. Silvertongue
43. 100 years old
44. Lyra
45. He is a murderer
46. A cat
47. Roger and Iorek
48. Lee Scoresby and
   Will's father
49. Nine or ten years
50. Roger van Poppel

QUIZ 10

1. Oxford
2. The alethiometer
3. Mrs Coulter
4. His servant, Thorold
5. Dr Mary Malone
6. Plum brandy
7. Three
8. A serpent
9. Eight
10. Edward Coulter

11. A canal boat
12. Iofur Raknison
13. Lizzie Brooks
14. Will
15. He dies
16. Kendal Mint Cake
17. The Chevalier Tialys
18. A harpy
19. Lee Scoresby
20. Roger

21. Twelve
22. Morocco
23. Cardinal Sturrock
24. Father Gomez
25. A sewing machine
26. The Chevalier Tialys's
    dragonfly

27. A child
28. Their dæmon
29. Gold
30. Sir Charles Latrom

31. Roarer
32. A priest
33. In a locket around her neck
34. The General Oblation
    Board
35. A pine-marten
36. Father Gomez
37. Lyra
38. Swan
39. Lyra
40. A cat

41. Jerry
42. A spear
43. Oxford
44. The goose-dæmon
45. Seth
46. The Prescient
47. Will
48. A gyptian
49. The Skraeling
50. The Steward

MEDIUM ANSWERS

QUIZ 11

1. Wine
2. Lord Roke
3. Will
4. *The Subtle Knife*
5. College of St Jerome
6. The harbour
7. Balthamos
8. By air
9. Water people
10. The General Oblation Board
11. Walrus ivory carvings, silver cups
12. She is hit by a motor vehicle
13. His arm
14. Three
15. It was the same sex as himself
16. The Porter
17. Six
18. Landloper
19. Jerry's
20. Lena Feldt

21. The Ministry of Theology
22. His helmet
23. Grumman
24. Valley of rainbows
25. Chewing gum, baked beans
26. Dr Malone
27. Sebastian Makepeace
28. A pistol
29. Farder Coram
30. Ama

31. A Rolls Royce
32. The Retiring Room
33. The mulefa
34. Lady Salmakia
35. Father Semyon
36. Gyptians
37. An osprey
38. Lyra
39. Jericho
40. Alaska

41. Metatron
42. John Faa
43. Protect against insects
44. Farder Coram
45. Alchemy
46. A fox
47. Children
48. Mrs Coulter
49. A snow leopard
50. Lee Scoresby

QUIZ 12

1. John Parry
2. Lord Asriel
3. The King of Lapland
4. Special Branch
5. Bamboo
6. Sebastian Makepeace
7. Coffee
8. Juta Kamainen
9. The Master
10. A walrus

11. Jared
12. A lute
13. Flour
14. Giant birds
15. Texas
16. In his waistcoat pocket
17. 36 symbols
18. The Himalayas
19. Pantalaimon
20. Lyra's

21. A human skull
22. Blue
23. His heart
24. Ruta Skadi
25. Six inches
26. False
27. John Parry,
    Stanislaus Grumman

28. Roger
29. A fire drill
30. She throws them into
    the furnace

31. The Chevalier Tialys and
    Lady Salmakia
32. Farder Coram
33. A knife
34. Tony Makarios
35. Lord Roke
36. A green leather armchair
37. True
38. Yes
39. Iofur Raknison
40. The Swiss Guard

41. Dr Payne
42. Coffee
43. A dog
44. Ruta Skadi
45. A cat
46. Farder Coram
47. Elaine
48. Lord Asriel
49. Reading his father's letters
50. The alethiometer

QUIZ 13

1. Tear it down
2. St Michael's
3. A wardrobe
4. Chevalier Tialys,
   Lady Salmakia
5. Nine years old
6. Marisa
7. A boy
8. He is owed money
9. Dr Cooper
10. Two sledges

11. Tigers (Snow-tigers)
12. Lord Asriel
13. Africa
14. The Parslows
15. Mrs Coulter
16. On Lee Scoresby's sledge
17. A bell
18. The University of
    Gloucester
19. Two missing fingers
20. Will Parry

21. A zeppelin (an airship)
22. Mrs Coulter's
23. King Ogunwe
24. Dust
25. There are humans bigger
    than them

26. The German Academy
27. Lord Boreal
28. The Oblation Board
29. A zeppelin
30. His left leg

31. Ama
32. The North Pole
33. The subtle knife's
34. The Master
35. Wildcats
36. One
37. Lord Asriel's forces
38. Red (rust-red)
39. Svalbard
40. The Tower of the Angels

41. His mother
42. Raymond van Gerrit
43. A hairpin
44. His left shoulder
45. The Fens
46. The Chevalier Tialys
47. Lyra's
48. Reindeer
49. Serafina Pekkala's
50. Beat Iorek in single combat

QUIZ 14

1. Mrs Coulter
2. Iorek Byrnison
3. The Imperial Muscovite Academy observatory
4. Ma Costa
5. The Chevalier Tialys
6. An angel
7. The Master
8. Lyra
9. Three
10. *The Subtle Knife*

11. Lord Asriel
12. Scholars
13. Lee Scoresby
14. Mrs Coulter
15. Benjamin de Ruyter
16. It was not Lyra's fault
17. St Sophia's
18. A hare
19. Teukros Basilides
20. A group of twelve

21. Fuel
22. The Tartars
23. False
24. Will Ivanovitch
25. Father Gomez

26. Ma Costa's bunk bed
27. Merton College
28. Metatron
29. Lord Roke
30. A witch's dæmon

31. Trollesund
32. Vodka
33. Iron fence bars
34. Jessie Reynolds
35. The subtle knife
36. Over 100
37. Always barred
38. Tualapi
39. A net
40. Starlings

41. Oak
42. Balthamos
43. A wolf
44. A bow
45. Pantalaimon
46. Thorold
47. Lord Roke
48. Tony Makarios
49. Two years
50. It can glow in the dark

QUIZ 15

1. Trollesund
2. Lee Scoresby's
3. A fire-hurler
4. To get some treacle toffee
5. Ratter
6. Eight
7. Serafina Pekkala
8. Rosewood
9. Will
10. 33,000 years

11. Lyra
12. A whale
13. Mrs Coulter's
14. Twelve
15. A tent
16. Serafina Pekkala
17. The Hall
18. Iorek
19. Blue
20. Sir Charles Latrom

21. His mother's bedroom
22. The Master
23. Roger
24. Carlo
25. A whistle
26. Father Gomez

27. Billy
28. Lyra
29. A dolphin
30. Prague

31. Indifferent
32. One day
33. Her shoe
34. Kitchen boy
35. Metatron
36. Serafina Pekkala
37. 300 years
38. Mrs Coulter
39. 17th Century
40. Farder Coram's dæmon

41. The Aurora
42. The alethiometer
43. No
44. Bloodmoss
45. Five
46. 20
47. They assume one form permanently
48. Metatron
49. A day
50. At the Experimental Station

QUIZ 16

1. The beehive
2. Lapland
3. Adults
4. North
5. Both legs broken
6. A library card
7. Nuniatak dig
8. Lord Asriel
9. Mrs Coulter
10. A hot-air balloon

11. Farder Coram
12. The Bible
13. Lord Asriel, the Master
14. An angel
15. Squadron No.2
16. Fell Press
17. Ama
18. His little finger
19. Benjamin de Ruyter
20. Lee Scoresby

21. Six
22. Will's
23. Storks
24. Mrs Coulter
25. Mrs Coulter
26. The millions

27. Stanislaus Grumman
28. A reindeer
29. Banbury
30. Lemonade

31. St Sophia's
32. The Church
33. A bruise on her cheek, make-up on only one eye
34. The Master
35. Eve
36. Mrs Coulter
37. The subtle knife
38. Ma Costa
39. Two
40. Black

41. Dr Lanselius
42. Wheels
43. A pistol
44. A pine marten
45. Tullio
46. For Lord Asriel
47. Four days
48. The city of magpies
49. Seven
50. Tokay

QUIZ 17

1. Serafina Pekkala
2. Dr Mary Malone
3. A can of cola
4. Father Gomez
5. Lee Scoresby
6. Gold
7. Siberia
8. No
9. A lifetime
10. A bear

11. An island
12. Cliff-ghasts
13. The Church
14. Fra Pavel
15. Lyra
16. Seal meat
17. Hornbeam trees
18. A journalist
19. A piece of rope
20. A grey dog

21. Clerkenwell
22. Will
23. Lord Asriel's
24. On Midsummer's Day
25. The man she had loved

26. Magician
27. To the canal
28. Stefanski
29. Father Makepwe
30. *Northern Lights*

31. John Faa
32. Sir Charles Latrom's
33. Three times
34. The witches
35. Iorek Byrnison
36. No-Name
37. The study
38. Father Gomez
39. Will's father
40. A gazelle

41. Lee Scoresby
42. The alethiometer
43. Seed pods
44. Two
45. London
46. Roger's
47. Thorold
48. Will
49. Mrs Coulter
50. Dæmons

QUIZ 18

1. Trollesund
2. Portugal
3. Lord Asriel
4. Right arm
5. Giacomo Paradisi, Lyra
6. The Authority
7. Kholodnoye
8. Short and stubby with black tape around it
9. Lord Asriel's spies
10. Iorek Byrnison

11. Lord Asriel's
12. His father
13. The Witch Counsel (Dr Lanselius)
14. Walters
15. Serafina Pekkala
16. Angels
17. Edward Coulter
18. Lyra
19. Angelica, Paolo
20. Lyra

21. Over 70
22. Lord Asriel
23. The German Ocean
24. Mrs Coulter

25. Lyra
26. A zeppelin (airship)
27. Lady Salmakia
28. A bearded seal
29. Lord Asriel
30. Yarnton

31. The spy-fly
32. Enoch
33. Iorek Byrnison
34. None
35. 1898
36. Moxie
37. Sir Charles Latrom
38. The gyptians
39. An ermine
40. One

41. Ruta Skadi
42. Ama
43. Gold
44. Iorek Byrnison
45. Lord Asriel
46. Muscovy
47. John Faa
48. Busy
49. A sledge
50. Sir Charles Latrom

QUIZ 19

1. Hester's
2. Mrs Coulter
3. The Master
4. Two
5. Nicholas Rokeby
6. The Sub-Rector
7. Two weeks
8. Two
9. Father MacPhail
10. Mary Malone

11. He killed another bear
12. Baruch
13. Angels
14. Burning the forest
15. False
16. Green
17. Iorek Byrnison
18. Torches
19. Will
20. Black velvet

21. Juta Kamainen
22. A priest
23. The gyptians
24. True
25. Kulang

26. The cat
27. Four thousand years
28. Two shillings
29. Six
30. The Chariot

31. The Magisterium
32. Serpent, crucible and beehive
33. Pantalaimon
34. A camel
35. The Cassington Scholar
36. A moth
37. The lodestone resonator
38. *The Amber Spyglass*
39. Chocolatl
40. Beans on toast

41. Lyra
42. The locket
43. Roger
44. The opposite sex
45. No
46. One
47. Cats
48. Molluscs
49. South
50. The zeppelin (the airship)

HARD
ANSWERS

1. The Master's
2. Hjalmur Hjalmurson
3. The hall table
4. Ma Costa
5. A hawk and a dog
6. A cup of tea
7. Yelena Pazhets
8. Madame Oxentiel
9. Ask a question
10. In the cellar of the priest's house

11. Ragi
12. Manganese and Titanium
13. Teukros Basilides
14. Gracious Wings
15. The subtle knife
16. Miss Greenwood
17. Dirk Jansen
18. 35
19. King Ogunwe
20. The corona

21. Xaphania
22. Kholodnoye
23. Lena Feldt
24. Beetroot soup
25. Dame Hannah Relf

26. The Master
27. Flying women
28. Five
29. Wren
30. Michael Canzona

31. 170
32. Ruth
33. Cedarwood
34. Sister Agnes, Sister Monica
35. Yambe-Akka
36. Sattamax
37. Wells Fargo Bank
38. Dr Polstead
39. He asked what was the first creature he killed
40. Sister Clara

41. The Pitt-Rivers Museum
42. Twelve
43. Sungchen
44. A serpent
45. Sebastian Makepeace
46. 1985
47. Mark Ransom
48. A fox
49. Teukros Basilides
50. A blackbird